He Ain't No Bum

He Ain't No Bum

BY O.A."BUM" PHILLIPS AND RAY BUCK
FOREWORD BY PAUL "BEAR" BRYANT

JORDAN
&
COMPANY
PUBLISHERS

Acknowledgements

That O.A. (Bum) Phillips is a down-home, old-fashioned man with some warm and worthwhile things to say is known to tens of thousands of die hard football fans in the City of Houston, State of Texas, and a large chunk of the rest of the country.

But it took a man like Jack Cherry to come up with the idea of a book on Bum and then to make that idea a reality.

Jack Cherry is the former public relations director of the Houston Oilers. He knows football, he knows Bum, and he knows people.

He also knows writers. Jack brought Ray Buck, the author, and Bum Phillips, the subject, together on this book. He arranged and scheduled their taping times, working in and around the hectic schedule of an NFL coach and a busy sportswriter, schedules he knows all too well.

He was the link between the coach, the writer, and the publishers, overseeing the important little details and keeping the project on track and on target.

We owe a special debt of gratitude to Jack Cherry for his thorough and capable assistance in the publication of this book.

We also owe a deep thanks to Lou Witt, who provided the photography, and to Margaret Wicke, who typed the entire manuscript.

Without their help, "He Ain't No Bum" would still be stored under that crew-cut hair beneath one of those trademark cowboy hats.

Jordan & Company, Publishers, Incorporated

**To Betty, Hallye, Hillary and Ryan
for keeping it all in perspective**

Library of Congress Catalogue Number LC 79-91290

ISBN Number 0-918908-14-0

Direct inquiries to:
Jordan & Company, Publishers Inc
214 40th Street
P.O. Box 814
Virginia Beach, Virginia 23451

**OTHER TITLES FROM
JORDAN & COMPANY, PUBLISHERS**

THE LOS ANGELES DODGERS: A Pictorial History

THE CINCINNATI REDS: A Pictorial History

THE PITTSBURGH PIRATES: A Pictorial History

THE BALTIMORE COLTS: A Pictorial History

THE WASHINGTON REDSKINS: A Pictorial History

THE WINNING TRADITION: A Pictorial History of Carolina Basketball

THE WORRELL 1000: One of Sailing's Most Demanding Races

THE PITTSBURGH STEELERS: A Pictorial History

DALLAS COWBOY CHEERLEADERS
1979-80 Official Publication of the Dallas Cowboys Cheerleaders

THE 1979 OFFICIAL BALTIMORE COLTS YEARBOOK

Contents

FOREWORD 13

INTRODUCTION. 15

Chapter I
I'D MAKE A GOOD ONE-TERM POLITICIAN 19

Chapter II
I NEVER DID LIKE THEM DRUGSTORE COWBOYS 27

Chapter III
FOUR THINGS I KNOW SOMETHIN' ABOUT 35

Chapter IV
THE COWBOY WHO FELL OFF A HORSE 41

Chapter V
IF TRADITION MEANS ANYTHING,
WE'RE GONNA AUTOMATICALLY LOSE. 43

Chapter VI
SIT A SPELL AND LISTEN UP 49

Chapter VII
BUMISMS 57

Chapter VIII
HOW TO SPIT TOBACCO IN A PUBLIC PLACE 61

Chapter IX
SEVEN RULES FOR COACHING FORTY-FIVE LARGE MEN 63

Chapter X
PEOPLE-WATCHING. 81

Chapter XI
WATCHING THE PEOPLE WATCHER 87

Chapter XII
IT'S HUMAN NATURE 91

Chapter XIII
THE STOIC QUARTERBACK 95

Chapter XIV
THE RENAISSANCE MAN. 103

Chapter XV
NO WAY YOU CAN PRACTICE BEIN' MISERABLE. 109

Chapter XVI
HE'S A JEKYLL AND HYDE 119

Chapter XVII
COUNTDOWN TO CATASTROPHE. 127

Chapter XVIII
THE BEHINDER WE GOT, THE WORSE IT GOT 135

Chapter XIX
A PARTY 141

Foreword

Bum was one of my assistants at Texas A&M in 1957, my last year there. He chewed that tobacco and had that dry wit. Well, our assistant coaches were all responsible for different areas to recruit, and Bum got every damn boy in his area. I don't remember if it was six or seven. I told him, "Bum, I'm going to give you a $500 bonus when I get it. I ain't got it right now." He thought I forgot it. But after I left and came over to Alabama, six or eight months later, I sent him five hundred bucks. I bet he was the most surprised fellow in Texas.

He has a great knack of handling people. They believe in him. If people think he's corny, well then, I'm corny. But I can't chew tobacco; it makes me sick. I tried it like the other boys, but I couldn't do it. By the time Bum came to me, I had already given up. Cigarettes had me by then. I used to have a bunch of cowboy hats, but gave them away. When I was at Kentucky, I wore one. In fact, I wore one in the Cotton Bowl one time.

Bum's a terrific individual with a lot of class. He's got a good football mind and, in his own way, he has a knack of selling, which is the same as coaching really. He handles the press well, the alumni well, the ticket-buyers well. He's a hard worker. But I imagine he's got some other people working now. He was a hard worker when he was with me at Texas A&M, but then I didn't do anything.

I'll tell you something else about him. I've been knowing him for many years, at least 30, and I have never heard anyone say anything about Bum Phillips that wasn't complimentary. That's a pretty good testimonial because coaches are an awful jealous bunch of people.

He's very honest and open with his players. When he first came to me, the players already respected him because he had a high school coaching record of 90-something-and-2 at Nederland, Texas. He coached a little of everything with me. He gave me a defense that we still use today. It's a numbers defense, terminology really. But by using numbers you can tell each man right where he lines up and what his responsibility is. We still use it at Alabama. You can have half of your front playing one thing and the other half playing another thing, and the secondary makes its call. There's nothing to it.

I remember one day when he first came to us. The kickers were on the field early and Bum was working with the center, when I just happened to walk out to the field. The team manager hadn't brought the balls out. Bum turned over to me and said, "We ain't got any balls out here. What are we gonna do about it?" I told him, "I don't know. I'm sure not going to go get them." So he went and got the balls. I think he expected me to be the ball boy, but I'm too old.

Bum is my good friend. He's been in the news and he'll be in it some more. I don't know that much about pro football and I don't see that much of it. But I think the Houston Oilers are going to be good a long time, as long as Earl Campbell keeps running the football.

And since he's gotten rich, he might feel sorry for me and send that $500 back.

Paul "Bear" Bryant
Head Football Coach
University of Alabama

October 1979

Introduction

At the risk of sounding presumptuous, Mark Twain would have rooted madly for the Houston Oilers. If for no other reason than Bum Phillips is a tireless story-teller who blends wit and wisdom into each down-home Texas yarn, mixing spoof with non-fiction, pausing to spit tobacco juice where punctuation marks belong, speaking from the heart and not just the head.

Oh, he hasn't revolutionized the National Football League; he has simply made it more fun to follow. I first met him via telephone in 1976 while covering the local NFL franchise for *The Cincinnati Enquirer* and needing another mid-week story prior to one of those biannual Bengal-Oiler events that usually end in a controversial call or improbable play. Bum was out on the field. Moments later, he returned my telephone call (himself, not his secretary) and graciously filled my notebook with some sit-a-spell humor about football and life. I was hooked. I desperately wanted Bum to get into a Super Bowl.

This book is not intended to formally chronicle his life but to share his honesty and his humor. It's not to tell you about a man's life, but to introduce you to the man. It is not a biography but a collection of quotes and anecdotes. Bumisms, so to speak. This is not an attempt to spell a legend but to provide a forum for a man who has something to say (with apologies to grammar teachers everywhere).

He has become a microwave coach, providing Instant Quotes. Stories and analogies are a very basic, and necessary, part of this straight-shootin', tobacco-spittin' cattleman from Orange, Texas, who entered the NFL in 1974 and has become one of its most colorful characters of all time. He wears cowboy hats (except inside domed stadiums) and exotic western boots (would you believe red anteaters?) and wouldn't be caught dead in an Yves Saint-Laurent three-piece suit.

There isn't a pretentious or deceitful bone in Bum's body. He thinks a "hustler" is the first player downfield on kickoff coverages. That's just the way Momma raised him.

The second time Bum and I met was in Houston late in the

'76 season. He invited me — an out-of-town sportswriter — to watch Saturday practice, which is about as commonplace in the National Football League as Al Davis hugging Pete Rozelle. NFL coaches have a way of trusting nobody outside their film room, especially *out-of-town sportswriters.*

"Your bein' here ain't gonna have a whole lot to do with the outcome of the game," Bum assured. This made me feel better immediately.

By the third time we met, Bum was already refusing to accept my formal handshake. "Friends don't shake hands," he drawled. "They just say, 'howdy.' "

Bum is from the old school. He still believes football should be enjoyed by the players and no game is World War III. He keeps a perspective as broad as an end sweep. Players love to play for Bum Phillips.

Over the years, especially through the '78 playoffs in which the Oilers made it to the championship round, Bum has been a delight to cover. Sportswriters don't write Bum Phillips stories; Bum Phillips stories write themselves.

And so the purpose of this book is to share the belly-laughs and the country philosophies of a football coach who took the long and winding road from Nederland (Texas) High School to the Houston Oilers. The surface of the road might have changed from hard-rock dirt to smooth-silk concrete, but the traveler hasn't.

That's one big reason why he ain't no bum.

Ray Buck
Cincinnati, Ohio

October, 1979

HeAin't
NoBum

I'd Make A Good One-Term Politician

His name was Jack Sanford, and he was one of those precocious kids who seem to grasp everything there is to know about tossing and catching and blocking and tackling somewhere between the cradle and kindergarten. By the time he reached high school, he could divide a defense and show-and-tell a triple-reverse hand-off better than anybody in his class at Nederland (Texas) High School. He was one of Bum Phillips' first super jocks.

But Jack was also young and rambunctious; Bum was inexperienced and stubborn. And to this day, Bum blames himself for mishandling the 17-year-old boy and, consequently, wasting a tremendous amount of football talent.

Bum, who has gone on to bigger things like coaching the Houston Oilers into the American Football Conference Championship Game last season, still has this melancholy flashback that haunts him every now and then.

Bum remembers poignantly, "Jack Sanford had a heckuva lot of ability. He was all-district and second team all-state his junior year, then he went out for track. But after three weeks, the track coach told me Jack was missin' workouts. So I went to Jack and told him, 'If you say you're goin' out for track, do it. Otherwise, you know the consequences. If you get kicked off the track team, you won't play football next fall.' "

It was a threat intended to scare the irresponsibility out of young Sanford. The more severe the punishment, Bum reasoned, the less perfunctory the child. But it didn't work that way. Jack Sanford, free of spirit, continued to be a regular no-show.

"So the track coach kicked him off the team," Bum recalls. "Next fall, Jack came sailin' in to pick up his football uniform and I told him no. He was off the team. So he quit school and went into the Navy."

Well, Bum's mouth dropped open and his heart nearly stopped. But a decision was a decision. He stuck to his guns, so to speak. Jack Sanford was gone. Life would go on.

"But I ain't afraid now to say I made a mistake," Bum laments. "If I had been smarter, I could've accomplished the same thing and it wouldn't have hurt either one of us, the team or the kid. But in those days, I thought once you committed yourself to somethin' you had to stay with it. I don't mind eatin' my words now.

"What did track have to do with football? I proved a point at someone else's expense. That was 1955 and I ain't done that again. If that's discipline, then I don't want discipline. You gotta allow for a fella to mess up every once in awhile."

Bum, who became the ninth head coach in the then 16-year history of the Houston Oilers on January 25, 1975, has learned to be more tolerant and appreciative and understanding and all those things that players look for in a coach. All he expects in return is a straight answer and an honest effort. He is old-fashioned that way. He lives by something called the Golden Rule. His world is up-front and laid-back. He likes to think a person can get more accomplished that way.

Don't misunderstand. Bum has never envisioned himself sitting in the Oval Office or running for governor of the Great State of Texas ("I don't even like talkin' about the Super Bowl"). But he has daydreamed about politics from time to time. It happens when he wonders how the United States government can send a man to the moon but cannot build a practical car at a sensible price to deliver affordable gas mileage.

"I can't understand it. They can put two men in a capsule and land it on the moon within 50 yards of where they want it, but they're not smart enough to make a car that gets a hundred miles to the gallon. There's a fuel shortage because they want it that way. They know the American public is gonna burn the same amount of fuel, no matter what, and just spend more money. Don't tell me any different.

"We're attackin' the damn thing from the wrong end. If they have to charge $1.00 a gallon, why not make it $1.50 a gallon and use the 50 cents to subsidize a project to build a car that gets 100 miles to the gallon. This way you're *doin'* somethin'. The other way, it's like pourin' money down a rat hole."

Bum Phillips, who is as much a straight-shooter as he is a plain-talker, shakes his ever-present cowboy hat from side to side and makes a guttural sound before stepping down from his soapbox.

"Now I'll probably get a lot of letters tellin' me how to coach."

Politics? Bum shrugs, "I'd make a good one-term politician. I'm afraid I wouldn't get re-elected, though, 'cause there ain't but one way to do somethin' and it's got nothin' to do with gettin' votes.

"I make decisions accordin' to what's right and what's wrong, not to keep my job. A politician can't do that. He's gotta make his decisions according to the votes. He knows it could cost him his job."

Of course, pro football coaches are subject to the same dependencies as politicians. However, Bum makes it a point not to think of the Houston Oilers' future in terms of the length of his contract.

"We don't go out lookin' for a bunch of 27- and 28-year-olds," he says. "I'd rather draft 21- and 22-year-olds who are gonna play 10 or 12 years, rather than just how long I could be here."

Bum is a realist who can see past the indigestion and heartburn of a team pizza party. He's down-home enough to prefer a can of cold beer over a chilled bottle of Cabernet Sauvignon. So it's pizza and beer, not caviar and wine, when Bum rounds up his players for a party.

"Everybody makes fun of these little chickenbleep parties," Bum says. "But don't tell me they're unimportant. I make sure a group from the offense and a group from the defense get together every now and then. You gotta remember, friendship is nothin' you can *take* from a guy. He has to *give* it. That means sometimes you have to take the first step.

"It isn't that the whites don't like the blacks or that the blacks don't like the whites. They're just more comfortable staying by themselves. That's why I think you should have the parties. Force 'em to mix."

No, this isn't a political issue. It's a football issue, regarding winning and losing.

Bum grew up humbly during The Depression. His first cowboy hats were hand-me-downs from his grandfather, who stuffed a little tissue paper here and there to make them fit the youngster. His jaw is jutting, unmistakably clean-shaven, and he still wears his hair the length of toothbrush bristles. He was born September 29, 1923, Oail Andrew Phillips, according to his birth certificate, although he was blessed with the sobriquet "Bum" because his sister, Edrina, stammered as a toddler.

"She was three when I was one," Bum recalls. "How are you gonna expect a little girl three years old who stammers to say "Oail" when a grown person can't even say it?" (The way to say it, for grown-ups and children, is O-L).

So Edrina tried to say "brother" but it came out "B-b-b-bum" and nobody ever corrected her, least of all Bum. "It's a nickname," he shrugs, "it ain't a description."

A native of Orange, Texas, Bum played high school football at Beaumont French under the late Elbert Bickell, attended Stephen F. Austin University and coached high school football at Nederland, Port Neches, Amarillo and Jacksonville, all in Texas. Later he coached under Bear Bryant at Texas A&M in 1957 but chose to stay in Texas rather than follow The Bear to the University of Alabama the following year.

Bum then coached at the University of Texas-El Paso (then Texas Western) for one year before being named defensive coordinator at the University of Houston under Bill Yeoman. In 1967, he left to join Sid Gillman with the San Diego Chargers and remained there until Gillman left in 1971. He was defensive coordinator at Southern Methodist University under Hayden Fry the following year when SMU had the best defensive record in the Southwest Conference. He served as defensive coordinator at Oklahoma State in 1973 before rejoining Gillman's staff with the Oilers the following season.

"My daddy hated football," Bum recalls. "I came home late one night and he asked me where I'd been. I told him football practice — this was high school — and he said, 'You quit that; you'll get your leg broke.' The next night, I came home late again and he asked me where I'd been. I told him football practice and he wore my butt out good. Next night, the same thing. He told me to lay down on the bed and he wore me out again. Next night, same thing, but this time he said, 'Okay, but if you get your leg broke just remember I told you so.' Daddy was like a lot of country people. All you were supposed to do was work."

His father is deceased, but his mother, Naomi, is 75 years old and lives in Vidor, Texas. "She is doin' fine," Bum says. "She listens to all the Oiler games but gets a little nervous. She turns on the radio and then goes in another room. If it gets the least bit hairy, she hides."

Bum has a simple philosophy about losing football games: "You don't want to get beat to start with . . . but when you get beat by somebody you don't like, that makes it double-bad. If you get beat by somebody you like, at least you got somethin' to feel good about."

When the Oilers' winningest season in nearly two decades ended on the short end of a 34-5 horror in Pittsburgh's Three Rivers Stadium last January, Bum didn't have to feel double-bad. "I like Terry Bradshaw and I respect the Pittsburgh Steelers," he could tell himself. It provided a measure of solace on the long airplane ride back to Houston that evening.

Bum has been asked what he would do for a living if he wasn't coaching football. He sits a spell, mulls the thought over a chaw of tobacco and slowly lifts those extra-wide shoulders of his. "I dunno," he says. "Teach first grade, I guess. Little biddy kids. You say 'boo' to them and they jump. And you don't have to fine 'em."

But he loves his job. "I consider my vacation to start July 2," he says. "My vacation is all durin' football, so I got the longest vacation of anybody. Last year was seven months long."

Bum likes people but resents social gatherings. He enjoys an occasional round of golf but would rather draw a bye than play in a celebrity tournament. He wants to help folks, be nice to folks, but not be used by folks. If he isn't asked to be grand marshal of another small-town parade the rest of his life, that will be fine with him.

Bum is gracious. He will give you the peacock feathers off his cowboy hat. However, there was a time that he refused to donate money to a charity because of a bad experience he had while stationed in the South Pacific with the U.S. Marine Corps during World War II.

"They used to sell cigarettes and candy to the service men, instead of givin' it away like they were supposed to. Later I found out that this was just an isolated case where I was stationed," Bum emphasized.

But he was still disillusioned, because of that one incident, with that particular charity in 1946 when he returned home and took a job with the Magnolia Oil Refinery. When advised to donate to the non-profit organization, a company tradition, Bum refused, asking instead to be able to donate to the Salvation Army. His supervisor at Magnolia said, "Sorry, no way," and Bum replied, "In that case, tell the man at the gate to have my check ready. I'm leavin'."

And Bum left.

It didn't matter that he had only a high school diploma and that his wife, Helen, was expecting their first child. It didn't matter that he didn't have a rich uncle to call.

"It was the principle of the thing," Bum reasoned. "I got in my pickup and left. I always turned one way and circled around to go home but, for some reason, I turned the other way that day. I drove past Lamar Junior College and saw a bunch of 'em out there practicin'. I stopped by the road and watched."

Ted Jeffries, the Lamar coach, noticed the interested bystander with wide shoulders and approached him. "You a football player?" he asked.

"I used to be," Bum replied modestly.

"Well, how would you like to play for me this year?"

Bum thought a moment. "I ain't got nothin' better to do."

So Jeffries saw to it that Bum received a $120-a-month scholarship under the GI bill, plus room, board and tuition fees. He was on his way to a career in football, compliments of a charitable organization.

"In the whole time that I've been coachin' — and I get a jillion letters from fans — I don't guess I've had three letters that have been critical. I've never met a fan in all the time I've been meetin' them that has said somethin' you wouldn't want to have said in front of your family. I enjoy fans. I guess I enjoy people.

There's a certain amount of pride in just havin' somebody want to know who you are or want to shake your hand. Hell, I'm human. I like for people to act like they know who I am."

Bum signed a three-year contract last January, two weeks after he led the Oilers to the AFC Championship Game and their first appearance in the playoffs since 1969. The only question anybody had about Bum's signing was, "What took Bud Adams so long?"

"There was never any problem, as far as I was concerned," Bum maintains. "I used to fight with my sister, and you know I love her. Bud and I get along good. I can call him right now and borrow money from him. There is only one coaching job I want, and I have it.

"Both of us agree. I'll be coaching here a long time or as long as Bud Adams wants me. I figure I'll be coaching only five, six, seven, eight years longer, so I'll be damned if I'm gonna spend five of those years with people I don't like just to prove a point."

This is your basic one-term politician. His message is as simple as his moniker. Just call him Bum. "As long as you don't put a 'you' in front of it," is all he asks.

*"All in all my years on the trail are the happiest I have lived
. . . Most of the time we were solitary adventurers in a great land
as fresh and new as a spring morning, and we were free and full
of the zest of darers."*

Charlie Goodnight, cowboy
Inscribed at the Museum of
Westward Expansion in St. Louis

I Never Did Like Them Drugstore Cowboys

Ever since he was old enough to pitch hay and ride a horse, Bum Phillips would rather spend an hour around the barn than sit through a Tom Mix double-feature at the local movie house. Celluloid cowboys were never his kick. He saw right through their pretty faces and primped kerchiefs.

"They were always kinda phony; that's why I really didn't care for cowboy shows," he recalls. "Now take John Wayne, Jimmy Stewart, Glenn Ford and Chill Wills, they were different. I could sit and watch them. They were real people.

"But Tom Mix, Roy Rogers and that crowd, they were a kind of drugstore type. That jumpin' onto a horse from behind can get your ribs broke or get you killed. First of all, that would take a whole lot of trainin' and then there ain't no horse gonna stand there and let somebody jump on her back from off a building.

"Gawdalmighty! I got one mare that I'd like to see somebody try and touch, much less straddle her. I'll give that hussy away if they can."

You don't fool Mother Nature or real cowboys. Bum's paternal grandfather was a Texas Panhandle cattleman named Joe Phillips, who worked a dozen years along the famous Charles Goodnight Trail during the 1870s.

Bum describes him warmly as "just a nice, plain ol' cowboy."

His maternal grandfather was Monroe Parrish, an executive type who operated the E. W. Brown Estate in Orange, Texas, for nearly 50 years.

"It was the oldest cattle range in Orange," Bum recalls. "My grandpappy ran it but he didn't own it. If he did, I wouldn't be coachin'."

Bum's father was Oail Andrew Phillips, Sr., but everybody called him "Flip" until the day he died. It was just easier to say with a mouthful of tobacco.

"My daddy was a dairyman, a truck driver, a lot of everything," Bum says. "He played baseball but he didn't care for football. He didn't think there was any future in it."

Tracing his roots, you can understand why this 56-year-old coach of the Houston Oilers doesn't feel terribly comfortable wearing a pair of Florsheim wing-tips and a Wembley tie.

His wife, Helen, is a sweet, white-haired lady who is equally as natural and delightfully uninhibited. She wears an oversized Earl Campbell T-shirt to feed the horses but makes no bones about Carl Mauck being her favorite Oiler player — "and you can quote me on that."

As the song goes, she stands by her man. That's Bum. "If you're lucky enough to marry a cattleman," she says, "a girl should do it. They're kind, gentle, considerate, and all cattlemen respect their women folk."

Bum has to agree. "That's 100 per cent right. It's just accepted. You don't curse around women. You're taught from the time you're a little kid that you respect them. Sometime when you go to a rodeo, look around. The ones who are cowboys will treat their women the way you'd want your daughter to be treated. Other kinds of cowboys will be poppin' off and cursin' and makin' fools of themselves. They're not cowboys; they're somethin' else."

Here is something about Bum that tells you he is a family man, without his pulling out the wallet photos. He walks around with peace of mind and believes in the traditional values, perhaps that's it. He has his son, Wade, working for him, and refuses to apologize about it. Maybe that is Bum's best asset — the ability to see right through things.

"It makes it kind of tough because both the father and the son lean over backwards to show there is no favoritism. But d'ya know the proudest thing I am of anything I've done in coachin' is that I hired my son as an assistant. He's a good coach and he's proved he's a good coach, and I didn't let the fact he was my son keep me from hirin' him.

"Way back when I was coachin' in high school, I said I was gonna play the one that deserved to play, no matter if he was the president of the school board's son or what. I've managed to stick to that. It's the only way you do it. At least it's the only way I can do it and live with myself," he says in a low, deep voice that seems to originate from the callouses on the bottoms of his feet.

Family life is very important to Bum, although he likes to joke about it.

"I take my wife everywhere with me," he says with a straight face, "because she's too ugly to kiss goodbye."

Bum isn't above using his weekly press conference as a forum for one of his jokes: "I have to tell ya'll about the lady who came up to me before the game. She said her husband had died and she wanted me to give his Oiler season ticket to someone. I asked her why she just didn't give it to one of his friends and she said, 'I would but they're all at the funeral.' "

Half the sportswriters took him seriously and started taking notes. Later Mike Lutz of the Associated Press wrote that it wasn't long ago that pro football in Houston was the subject of the jokes; now the Oilers are telling them.

"The Houston Oilers were the joke of the National Football League in 1972 and 1973 when they put together consecutive 1-13 seasons," Lutz wrote. "The critics' standard line . . . was that the Oilers were doing okay; they won one game in 1972 and came right back with another victory in 1973. Now it's the Oilers who are telling jokes."

Bum has been described as a Will Rogers clone. He has a story for every occasion and an occasion for every story. He hasn't met an Earl Campbell he doesn't like. When this book was being planned, Bum informed Darrell Royal at the University of Texas that somebody would be contacting him for assistance.

"P.S. Probably won't be over three pages unless I lie a lot," Bum scribbled at the bottom.

In reality, all he has to do is talk. "The pros are boys just like high school players," he will tell you. "They're just older boys, that's all."

About coaching the B-squad at Nederland High School, he says, "I think you learn somethin' in that atmosphere, where you have to teach 'em how to tie their shoes and everythin'."

Bum can spot a counterfeit a country mile away. It's one of those inherent traits from an era of American history when cowboys were "free and full of the zest of darers." Something inside Bum tells him John Wayne was perhaps the perfect cowboy.

"He was a symbol," Bum says as if stating a fact, rather than delivering a eulogy. "He was what I thought a cowboy ought to be like. He was fair to everyone and he didn't dress up pretty. In the movies, he was always killin' the Japs and savin' the wagon train. I either liked him or the guy who wrote his scripts.

"I think he was something like he was portrayed, at least that's what I've always heard. He didn't act; he reacted. He wasn't a put-on."

Bum has this undying respect for unpretentious people. Like Toni Fritsch. Now Toni is about as natural as wheat germ. He is Bum's kind of people, and one can only wonder what kind of cowboy he would've made if he had grown up in Austin instead of Austria.

Fritsch is the side-winding, stomach-protruding, 34-year-old place-kicker of the Oilers. Bum loves him. "He's comical without meanin' to be comical," Bum says. "He's different. He can joke on hisself."

Bum has a graphic way of describing Fritsch's physique, knowing full well that Toni isn't sensitive about the shadow he casts. "It looks," Bum muses, "like a whole Dutch family moved out of the seat of them pants.

"But how he looks don't bother him. Pants are just somethin' to cover his legs. He ain't interested in modelin' out there on the football field."

Unpretentious isn't the only quality that Bum admires in Fritsch, who was acquired as a free agent in 1977 after spending 5½ years with the San Diego Chargers and Dallas Cowboys. He has given Oiler fans a foot they can trust.

"He can kick the ball better than anybody I've ever seen," Bum praises lavishly, Texas-style. "I mean he's got more touch than anybody I've ever seen. He's brimmin' with confidence. He just knows he's gonna make everything he kicks. There's no doubt in his mind. Some people *hope* they do; he *knows* he will.

"We brought him down here to work him out in 1977 about halfway through the season, and he started kickin' real close, about the 10-yard line. He stepped up there and boop! He dumped it over the bar by about five or six feet. He went back to the 20-yard line and boop! He dumped it over the bar about five or six feet again.

"I thought to myself, 'He's not gonna have enough leg when we get back to the 40.' Well, we kept movin' back five yards at a time and he dumped it over the bar by about five or six feet every time. Come to find out, that's his touch. He just kicks the ball over the bar, that's all. Most of them kickers will try one from the 10-yard line and like to knock it out of the park.

"I've never seen one like Toni. He comes out to practice and bets you that from the 20-yard line he can hit the crossbar one out of five times and, if you really crowd him, he'll bet you he can do it *two* out of five times. But don't bet him. He's won quite a few dollars out there.

"He's the only guy that I've ever seen that can kick a football so well that he'll practice *missin'*. He'll practice shootin' at the damn crossbar or practice hittin' the upright or practice hittin' the very top of the upright. He'll put it anyplace he wants to put it. He'll come out and kick sometimes 40 or 50 in a row, then when that gets monotonous he'll practice hittin' the crossbar for awhile. It don't bother him to miss."

But kickers are viewed as freaks by some. Many professional football players, especially those who are required to fight past a 260-pound guard and a 265-pound tackle before they can hopefully daze a quarterback, have the opinion that field goal specialists are to pro football what rodeo clowns are to the rodeo. Kickers usually speak two or three different languages, avoid contact at all cost and don't know a headslap from a quarterback sneak.

"I consider kickers to be football players," Bum reckons. "In a 10-7 ball game, one of 'em is the difference."

It is Bum's belief that specialization should never be allowed to disrupt team unity. The Houston Oilers practice esprit de corps. They sweat together; they drink beer together; they wear cowboy hats together; they once even helped Dan Pastorini move from one apartment to another. Everybody pitched in, including the head coach.

Bum has one unbreakable law: "Can't be nobody outside the team." That goes for rodeo clowns and field goal kickers alike.

It begins with Bum making the 45th Oiler on the team feel as important and as comfortable as Earl Campbell or Curley Culp. He understands a man's pride and feelings and psyche and ego, and that's why such a time-honored ritual as clocking players in the 40-yard isn't observed in Houston.

Bum doesn't own a stop watch.

"What do you have to time Billy Johnson or Kenny Burrough for?" he asks. "They're fast enough."

Bum is something of an NFL iconoclast, but in a palatable sort of way. His personality greets you ahead of his opinions. He is a man of strong convictions and no pretenses. In other words, he is as easy to listen to as dentist-chair music and he gets his message across without blitzing.

The fat has been trimmed off his philosophies. The window dressing is gone. Superfluous testing and meaningless numbers have been junked.

"What does timing somebody prove?" Bum asks again. "Okay, some guys ain't as fast as other guys. But we can't say, 'We're gonna time you-all but we ain't gonna time you,' because that makes it look like we don't trust you-all. If they're on your team, they're on your team. You can't let 'em think anything different for a second."

There is a sensitivity and urgency for togetherness about Bum that can be traced to his childhood. He grew up during The Depression. He wasn't spoiled by material gifts, just coddled by kin.

"We were poor-poor," he recalls. "Poor in the sense of money but rich in many other ways. Daddy drove a truck from Beaumont to Houston twice a day, 16 to 18 hours a day, six days a week. He did that seven straight years without missing a day.

"He never asked nobody for nothing. That was his job and that's what it took — two trips a day. He couldn't make a livin' by doin' it only once. We didn't have any money; but then, nobody around us had any.

"That's why I don't believe people who say, 'You better chaperone your kid, take him fishin' all the time or he'll grow up wrong.' I'd see my daddy only every now and then because he was workin'. If it comes down to makin' a livin' and bein' a buddy to your kid, you better make a livin' or you won't have a kid to be a buddy to.

"My daddy didn't work on Sunday, so we usually went to the creek for a fishfry. The men played dominoes and the women cleaned the fish. It probably didn't cost five bucks to feed all 20 or 25 people in the immediate family. We had fun. We didn't know anything else. We didn't know there was a Disneyland."

But now that he knows there's a Disneyland, Bum really hasn't changed much. Success, financial security, even NBC-TV closeups haven't affected his hat size or altered his principles.

"I don't go throwin' away Bud Adams' money, either," he says. "You don't go wastin' something just because you can. I treat Bud Adams' money like it was mine. When I was growin' up, I didn't realize we was poor, so I guess that's why I've never been envious of what other people have. They can have what they have."

Bum has a heritage that was nurtured along the Charles Goodnight Trail a century ago and depicted by John Wayne on the movie screen. That is what *he* has. And that is unique to the fraternal order of NFL coaches.

Four Things
I Know Somethin' About

The 1979 stretch-cab pickup screams down the six-lane highway that leads Bum out of Houston to his suburban home in Missouri City, 45 minutes from the Astrodome on a good traffic-weaving afternoon.

This cowboy flies.

He likes to keep the speedometer needle stuck at 65, until some dinky compact clogs the passing lane. Bum chews, simply lifts his right cowboy boot, cranks the steering wheel right-left-right, plants his right cowboy boot once again and resumes 65. Earl Campbell doesn't do it any better on AstroTurf.

Waylon Jennings can be heard agonizing the words to *House of The Rising Sun* on the eight-track, and the head coach of the Houston Oilers is back in his saddle again. He plays his music the way he drives. Hard. He doesn't sing along because he doesn't believe in ruining a good thing.

"It's much easier to listen to somebody that can already do it than listen to myself tryin' to learn," he reasons. "I can't dance a lick, either."

On a good day, he has enough time and enough hands to keep Waylon Jennings and Willie Nelson tapes playing nonstop, first one and then the other, as if he is trying to arrive at a conclusion. Which is better? Waylon or Willie?

"Willie," he replies without hesitation. "But I wouldn't leave the room if either of 'em was playin'."

Bum is your basic homespun, set-a-spell, down-to-earth Texan who learned harmonica, defensive line and how to bulldog a steer all at about the same time in life. He's a cowboy at heart and a football coach in the public eye, one who does his homework but never lets the X's and O's get in his way of understanding folks.

"I don't care if people think I'm dumb," he says with a mischievous wink behind those wire-rimmed, rose-tinted glasses. "But I ain't gonna prove it for 'em."

He brought the "34" defense, three down linemen, four standing linebackers to Houston, traded for the 1978 draft rights to Earl Campbell (1,450 yards rushing as a rookie) and assembled a team that reached the championship game of the AFC playoffs in only his fourth season. Lest we forget, Bum inherited a 7-7 team that had been 1-13 and 1-13 before that.

But he is the same Bum who coached Nederland High School 25 years ago. He is the same Bum about whom Jack Gallagher of the *Houston Post* wrote a dozen years ago: "When he wears a single-breasted coat, as he did the other day, he buttons all three buttons, which should tell you something about his sartorial elegance. Bum is the cracker-barrel type, spouting homilies and apologetically explaining himself as an ol' country boy, meanwhile outslicking the city slickers. Of course, he learned the rural approach at the feet of The Master, P.W. (Bear) Bryant."

Bum, himself, likes to say, "There are four things in life I know somethin' about: pickup trucks, gumbo, cold beer and barbecued ribs." That's his biggest boast. That also explains the bulge around his middle and the diesel smoke that spews from the rear of his pickup. He loves to eat and hates to wait in any kind of line. He installed an extra 90-gallon tank on his pickup and stocked 500 gallons of diesel fuel at his horse stables.

"Hardest thing for me to do is sit in a barbershop and wait for a haircut," he confesses. "I won't do it. If I go by the barbershop and somebody's in the chair, I'll just keep goin' down the road. I ain't gonna stand in line to eat or get a haircut. Therefore, I get real hungry and my hair gets long sometimes."

Bum is a man's man. He leaves the family Cadillac for his wife to drive. But then Helen has always been cruise-control and rich Corinthian leather; Bum, four-wheel drive and washable vinyl. She is the former Helen Wilson from Bum's hometown of Orange, Texas, where they were considered by many to be an unlikely match. Bum was a cowpoke; Helen, a banker's daughter from the brighter side of town. But they were in love and announced their intentions to wed.

A Wilson relative is known to have sneered, "It's a plow-horse marrying a racehorse."

When out-of-towners asked Mr. Wilson who his beautiful

daughter was planning to wed, the highly respected banker replied, "She's marrying some farmer."

Bum and Helen Phillips laugh about it now. "Your daddy could've said *rancher*," he says. "Both of 'em would've been right."

The marriage worked, producing six handsome, healthy children — one boy and five girls, well spaced, ages 32 to 12. "The first one was a boy (Wade, an Oiler assistant coach) and I thought I was a winner," Bum says with a straight face, ". . . then along came five girls."

But having babies isn't one of the four things in life that he professes to know something about.

Gumbo is.

Take it from Bum, there isn't a better bowl of seafood gumbo served in the United States than the gumbo they serve up at Capt. Benny's on South Main in Houston. The place is a converted fishing boat, sits among a row of burlesque houses, seats about 15, stands about 25, offers no atmosphere, and stays busy until Capt. Benny closes the doors and shuts off the lights.

"People who know how to make good gumbo know that it's how you make the roux, the gravy," Bum explains. "Everything is added to that. Now I like lots of roux with just rice and seafood, rather than lots of tomatoes and okra and all that other stuff thrown in. I never made gumbo myself. But I guarantee I know somethin' about it. I promise you."

Naturally, you can't spoon a bowl of gumbo without tipping a can of cold beer. Aside from beer and water, Bum is a nondrinker. "I don't like the taste of anythin' other than beer," he says. "I don't smoke, either, for the same reason. I don't like the taste of cigarettes. I try a cigar about once a year, because every now and then I see somebody smokin' a cigar and it looks like they're enjoyin' it, so then I try one. I just re-prove to myself that I don't know what the hell anybody gets out of a cigar."

His favorite beers are Coors and Budweiser. Fancy German beers he abhors. "Too sour," he complains. "I'll drink most beers and they don't have to be cold. I drank a lot of warm beer when I was overseas. There wasn't a whole lot of ice available. In fact, that's where I first started to drink beer. I never drank it when I was a kid. An athlete wasn't supposed to do that."

But perhaps most of all, Bum is a connoisseur of barbecued ribs.

"There're two kinds," he explains. "There's the true barbecue, where you take meat and cook it slowly over an open fire; the other is where you just cook the meat in barbecue sauce to give it the flavor. But I'm a better eater than I am a cooker."

Bum's trademark is not his ribs. He is known instead for his Western hats and cowboy boots. His wardrobe stands alone in the National Football League. "A cowboy hat has a practical purpose, too," he says. "Take a look at the visitors' benches around the league; they put you lookin' into the sun."

Inside the Astrodome, however, Bum takes off his hat. He was brought up right. "Momma always told me never to wear a hat indoors."

But the 50,000-seat Astrodome?

"When it can't rain on you, you're indoors," he reasons.

Bum has a favorite hat shop in downtown Houston. A giant sign painted on the side of the building shouts at you: "Welcome To Houston, Home Of Gary's American Hats." When Bum shops there, he turns every head in the place, from clerks to clientele. "I've been buyin' hats there since 1946," he says. "I remember the first one I bought. A black one. Cost me $12. I'll never forget that hat."

That's quite a statement considering Bum buys between eight and ten felt hats in the winter and between eight and ten straw hats in the summer. He's a hat-a-holic. To make room in his house, he cleans out his closets and gives the old hats to assistant coaches with the same size head. Bum is one of those in-between sizes that haberdashers hate. He's smack between 7 and 7 1/8. "Except after a big win," teases salesman Richard Wolf, "then he's a 7 1/4."

Bum usually settles for light colors (although never pastels) and always a Rodeo Cowboy Association crease. He used to wear a butterfly crease which resembles the mouth of a Muppet. An RCA crease is plain in front and four-cornered on top.

"All brims come four inches wide," the salesman goes on to explain. "The bigger the person, the more brim we leave. With

Bum, we leave the full four inches."

"Yeah," Bum says dryly, "all the fat ones need four inches."

Bum's favorite bootmaker, Sandy Sanders of El Paso, is just as particular with fitting his size 12 feet. For example, it takes one anteater to make one boot and, if the pair were sold retail, the asking price would be $400 or more. "I just wish he'd get rid of that cowboy hat," Sanders grouses. "It makes him look like an 80-year-old bulldogger."

Bum's square-jawed, bespectacled face adorns several billboards throughout the state, promoting his bootmaker friend: "Sanders Is My Boot." The endorsement is invaluable.

"Shoot," Bum says without an inkling of pretense in his voice, "Sandy gave me boots way back when I couldn't help him none at all."

Bum requires two closets at home just to keep his boots. There is a linen closet in the hallway outside the master bedroom that has been overtaken by alligators and lizards and, most recently, eels. Nowhere else in the country, perhaps, do a powder blue anteater and a red kangaroo have so much in common.

Take a peek in Bum's boot closets. The assortment is staggering: two pairs alligator (one brown, one tan); two pairs anteater (one black, one powder blue); one pair beaver (dark brown); one pair caribou (dark brown); four pairs lizard (two sand, one brown, one honey); three pairs kangaroo (two red, one black); nine pairs ostrich (three powder blue, two bone, one gray, one honey, one brown, one blue-and-white patchwork); one ostrich leg (blond), and several pairs of more conventional leathers. He has smooth cowhide and roughouts, dress boots and knock-around boots.

Among the latest additions to his boot collection are three pairs of eel (one dark brown, one gray, one honey) and two pairs of crocodile (one gray, one blue). "Crocodile is different from alligator," Bum informs. "Crocodile skin has little squares with a little biddy spot in each square."

Sanders was sending Bum a sample pair of wild turkey, not the booze but the boot, as just another chance for Bum to be the first NFL coach on his block to wear something other than wingtips to the press conferences.

"My favorite boot is still ostrich," Bum says, reminding that ostrich leg is not the same as ostrich for reasons that are self-explanatory. "You can wear ostrich as dress or work. I like 'em because they give. Some of the other leathers are stiff.

"I don't know how many boots I got. But I got more than I can wear, I know that. I only got two feet."

There is a right boot without a mate that Bum has kept through the years. One side has a two-inch gash in it from a time Bum was helping a friend castrate cattle and was gored by a bull that objected to the indignity of the operation.

"Ruined that mother," says Bum, displaying the boot with a wry grin.

Helen Phillips has her own favorite story about Bum's footwear. "I knew Bum when he wore a pair of shoes once," she begins.

"Once?"

"Yes, once," she replies, "the day he got married." (They were black shoes.)

A warm, tranquil smile breaks across her face. "You've heard of men dying with their boots on. Well, I think Bum was *born* with 'em on."

Bum just sits there. Maybe he was. He can't refute it.

The Cowboy
Who Fell Off A Horse

Cowboys ain't easy to love and they're harder to hold,
They'd rather give you a song than diamonds and gold,
Mamas don't let your babies grow up to be cowboys
'Cause they'll never stay home and they're always alone,
Even with someone they love.

There was the day Bum fell off his horse.

Don't laugh because this ain't supposed to be funny. It was one of those times — believe it or not — when Bum was speechless. He was too busy trying to catch what had to be his last breath of life, he was sure.

It was the spring of 1977. His daughter, Kim Ann, 10 years old at the time, was petrified to see her daddy lying there on the ground, writhing in pain, grasping his left side, after being thrown from his horse and landing on a cement culvert beside the road.

Four ribs were broken, not cracked, but broken in two. His appendix was ruptured, Bum wanted to cry. Kim Ann wanted to cry. They both had reasons to cry because they were stranded in No Man's Land, and Bum couldn't even warn Kim Ann about the dogs if she should wander up to a farm house asking for help. It hurt too much to do anything but lie there and suffer.

"I knew if she went, those dogs would eat her up," Bum recalls. "But I couldn't talk, I just couldn't talk."

About then, as if Warner Brothers had written the script, Bum was rescued. Gene Dinges, one of Bum's cow partners and presumably wearing a white cowboy hat, happened to be hauling some bulls in a truck when he came upon the scene of the accident. Carefully, he helped Bum into his truck and drove him ever so gingerly over the dirt roads to a hospital where the ribs could be treated and wrapped.

"I still remember Gene drivin' about two or three miles per hour all the way to the hospital," Bum says appreciatively. "Let me tell ya, I couldn't stand them bumps in the road."

Bum played football in high school and college, he went through World War II, and he even rode horses that had never been broken. But this was his very first broken bone — and he had four of them.

"I was embarrassed as the devil," Bum remembers, while getting a little crimson around the crewcut. "I had ridden her 20 to 25 times and she hadn't jumped. But something spooked her. I didn't expect her to jump and she just did."

Of course, while convalescing, Bum heard from many of his buddies. Did he ever.

"I thought that if you had the hat and the boots, it meant you could ride a horse," was the tone of most of the mail from friends with a sharp needle.

CHAPTER V

If Tradition Means Anything, We're Gonna Automatically Lose

Don't try to sell Bum on tradition.

To him, it's just one of them fashionable nine-letter words that looks good on poster paper and sounds impressive in the locker room. But to some, it feels so good to say it. In fact, it carries the same social connotation as *designer label* and *sex appeal*. In America, it's chic to have it.

"Tradition don't mean anything," Bum scoffs. "Now *confidence* means something. I mean doin' it yourself. If tradition means anything, we're gonna automatically lose because our tradition is terrible."

When Bum came to the Oilers in the spring of 1974 as Sid Gillman's defensive coordinator, he was joining the most depressed football franchise in the National Football League. The Oilers were coming off consecutive 1-13 seasons in which they had been outscored by the opposition 827-363.

Bill Peterson was fired five games into the 1973 season and left with a 1-18 record, only to be succeeded by Gillman, who lost eight of the last nine games doing it his way. On January 18, 1974, Gillman announced that he would remain as general manager and head coach for at least one more season, ending speculation that a new head coach would be named.

On March 7, Bum joined the staff. On October 22, Curley Culp (and a No. 1 draft choice) was acquired from Kansas City for John Matuszak (and a No. 3 draft choice), giving the Oilers the fulcrum they needed on defense. On December 15, Houston defeated Cleveland for the first time ever and finished the season 7-7, its best record since 1968.

Happy New Year. The Oilers were beginning to feel good about themselves when O.A. (Bum) Phillips, defensive coordinator of the Oilers, was named head coach by Gillman.

Gillman assured everyone that a "good system" had been established and he would continue to oversee the operation as general manager. Three weeks later, he left the Oilers by mutual consent with owner Bud Adams. Suddenly, Bum had a hyphenated title with the letters "GM" in front of "head coach."

"We probably work as hard now as anybody works in practice," Bum says. "But the first year I was here as head coach, we had some people that didn't have good work habits. If we would've really tried to go at it hard, we would've had a lot of resentment."

"Mutiny" might have been a better description.

Bum, however, recognized a very combustible situation. The temperature in Huntsville, Texas, in mid-July and August hangs around 98 degrees and the humidity never drops below 90 per cent. It's a three-shirts-a-day town.

"If we really pushed them," Bum recalls, "we would've had half of them in the hospital."

But he took it easy on them for another reason, too.

"They didn't know me. They didn't know if I could coach or not. The fact that I said I was a coach didn't mean I'm a coach. They didn't know whether I could coach and I didn't know whether they could play.

"Sid was a driver. He had them on the field sometimes three hours at a time. That was him. I didn't have a chance to convince them, 'Look, here's why we gotta do this.' I was an assistant coach they didn't know from Adam."

Bum won't say it but Gillman was often criticized for sweating his team into shape early. They'd win games in September and October, then fade down the stretch.

The 1975 Oilers opened the regular season with a 7-0 victory over New England as Willie Germany returned a first-quarter fumble for a touchdown. Bum was an instant success.

The Oilers went on to defeat Washington for their first-ever win over a National Football Conference opponent, whip Kansas City for the first time since 1967, and score on the final play of the game to nip Oakland, 27-26, for the first victory over the Raiders since 1966.

Bum finished 10-4. It was the Oilers' winningest season since 1962.

"If we would've pushed them in Huntsville, we wouldn't have had a good year," Bum maintains. "But by winnin' that first year, they believed a little bit more the following year. It came out good so I guess that was the right way to do it."

For whatever credit Bum Phillips received for taking the Oilers to the AFC Championship Game last January, he can never receive enough for handling his players since he took the job.

"To me," he says, "the name of the game is getting your guy to do the best he can do. On every team, you got probably eight mediocre players and eight good players; all the rest of 'em are average. If you can get that average group — let's say half of 'em, 10 of 'em, even eight of 'em — moved up into the good category, you've improved your football team a helluva lot. Same goes with the mediocre players moved up into the average category.

"Our bunch ain't pretty dancers," Bum muses, "but we like 'em to dance every dance with everything they got."

He reached the AFC Championship Game with 21 free agents on the 45-man roster. That's 21 castaways, lost causes, somebody else's discards.

"I'm kind of a free agent myself," Bum says. "Besides, I don't think there's that much difference in talent. I think there's enough football players in this country that can play professional football. I'm a believer that coachin' is still important. I think there's still a place in football for coachin' and for drillin' and for motivatin' and for doin' things.

"A guy who signs for the big bucks is in trouble if he sits back and waits for the good times to start rollin' in. Because I don't care who makes our team. It can be a fourth-round draft choice or a twelfth-round draft choice, I could care less," Bum believes.

He does not subscribe to the theory that today's pro football player is a selfish, spoiled, slothful lout that signs a $75,000 contract with assorted bonuses and gives $1.98 worth of effort in return. On the contrary, he believes today's player is more dedicated than ever to keeping in peak physical condition.

"Salaries are so high now," Bum explains, "that players are makin' sure they stay in shape. In the past, you could quit football and go out and get a job payin' a comparable salary. Not today. Players want to hold on to what they have, so they work harder at stayin' in shape."

He understands that desire and ambition wear out long before arms and legs. A pro football player will remember the plays long after he grows sick and tired of the practices. But the money has a way of making it all tolerable.

"If the incentive is there, a man will stay in shape all year," Bum maintains, "and the incentive is there with the high salaries.

· "Then it's the job of the coach to get the player to know what you expect of him. Make *him* want to do it. When he's 21 years old, football is an eight-month-a-year job; when he's 25, it should be 10-month-a-year, and when he's 30, he better be working out year-round.

"Keepin' in shape is so important. If you take a shot in the arm and you've been liftin' weights, it's a bruise. If you haven't been workin' out, it can be a dislocated shoulder. A player shouldn't take a chance of losin' his job just because he didn't stay in shape. If you're alive, you might as well be workin' out."

An athlete is usually the last to know when his faculties have deteriorated beyond the minimum daily requirement. He hangs on. He can't practice but he can play. It is usually embarrassing to the player and burdensome to the team.

"You try not to let your football team age at the same time," Bum says. "No. 1, you try to keep your job long enough to be able to do something about it. I don't know what happened at Green Bay when Vince Lombardi left. But if Vince had stayed there, Green Bay never would've went down.

"Not that the people that came along (Phil Bengston and Dan Devine) couldn't coach. It's just that Vince built it and, it seems to me, if he stayed there in coachin', he would've foreseen the fact that (Jerry) Kramer or (Paul) Hornung or (Jim) Taylor was gettin' a little old. Instead, everybody wore out at the same time. Baltimore did the same thing. Good ones won't do that."

Herein lies a lesson in tradition.

"Green Bay's tradition is based on what (Bart) Starr and Kramer and Hornung and Taylor did. Now take Pittsburgh's tradition — that's based on what them guys playin' now have done.

There's a helluva difference.

"In other words, Green Bay's players today can't draw on the fact that Green Bay in 1965 was good. They've got to prove *they* are good. Pittsburgh *is* good."

To Bum, the difference is winning the Super Bowl and finishing third or fourth in the NFC Central. So much for tradition.

Sit A Spell
And Listen Up

He casually spits tobacco juice into make-shift receptacles (empty Gatorade cups work nicely) between easy-listening sentences about no-nonsense philosophies concerning football and life. His thoughts are incredibly lucid. He defines things in uncomplicated terms.

"Two kinds of football players ain't worth a damn," Bum says. "One that never does what he's told and the other that never does anything *except* what he's told."

It's the Mother Bird Theory. Bum will instruct and encourage and brag on a guy until the very last drop of ability is coaxed out of him. But Bum won't baby-sit forever. There comes a time when the player must leave the nest.

"I ain't no driver. My idea has always been to try and convince a guy *why* you do somethin'. I'd rather go at it from the standpoint of doing enough preparation mentally with him to make him aware when he's not doin' the best he can do. Then let *him* motivate hisself, because he's the guy that's gonna have to motivate hisself in the last quarter when he's hot and tired and behind. When you get your football team in the right frame of mind, you don't ever have to worry about driving 'em.

"If they're doin' it because you're makin' them do it, they're not gonna do near as good a job anyhow. You take a guy that's plantin' corn for a prison and take a guy in the next field plantin' his own corn. See who's got the best crop?

"That's what you gotta make it look like. Like it's *you*. It's *your* team. You're the guy who determines how far the team goes, not by me drivin' you.

"Besides, I don't know anybody in this league you gotta kick in the tail because I don't know anybody who's gonna much stand for it all the time."

Bum's method of coaching is just as much predicated on *what not to do* with a player as *what to do* with him.

"Sometimes we get coaching so hard that we overcoach.

Football's an automatic-reflex game. It's a game that if you do it well, you don't have to think about it. Where you get into trouble is a guy havin' to think.

"That's why rookies have a hard time makin' it. They don't have enough time to get their habits so doggone ingrained in them. They get so tied up with the technique you're tryin' to teach 'em that they don't get into the block. Then it looks like, boy, he's not tryin'. He *is* tryin' but he's thinkin'.

"You can overcoach a guy a helluva lot easier than you can undercoach him. I've seen more players overcoached than under-coached. The name of the game is tackle the guy with the ball. All that other stuff, like how you get there to tackle him, is immaterial as long as you get it done."

Bum isn't advocating freelance football. He has certain text-book techniques that he gets across to his players, but it's the way he gets them across that is important.

"Tell a guy what you want," he explains. "Tell him, 'I want this guy over here tackled,' or 'I want that guy over there blocked.' But don't go through a 30-minute lecture on how you want him to step. Let him try and do it *his* way.

"Then, like playin' golf or anything else, don't give him a jil-lion things to change. Give him *one* thing to change. 'Keep your head up this time and do the same thing.' Don't tell him, 'Keep your head up, get your feet apart, keep your base moving.' Don't give him 17 things."

Bum coached San Diego's All-Pro defensive tackle Louie Kelcher at San Diego State and quickly recognized that Louie was a candidate for overcoaching.

"All of us teach technique. But technique to Louie Kelcher in college was not important at all because he was stronger and big-ger and better than anybody he was playin' against. As long as he's doin' better than everybody else, you don't bother a guy with technique.

"I mean when Louie came out of college, he ran the 40-yard dash in 5.2 or 5.3 seconds, but that was with an offensive guard in front of him or by hisself. It didn't make no difference. He went right on through the guy. That's what I liked about Louie Kelcher."

The Oilers achieved the playoffs last season for the first time since 1969 and Bum was awarded, after a strange delay, a three-year contract. It came January 22, nine days before his existing two-year contract was scheduled to expire.

Herein lies the single most distinguishable change in the man, according to long-time friend and assistant coach Eddie Biles. "A degree of change that anyone would go through," says Biles. "I mean he feels the pressure of coaching a little more than he did five years ago."

Bum nods. It's a fact of coaching. "Them two-year contracts are hard to live with. You have to do what it takes for the good of the football team and also have some time to spend with your family. It's hard to rassle with sometimes."

"I was gonna coach for a couple of years, you know, get it out of my system, then go back to the oil fields or buy a farm someplace. My idea of a permanent job was to hire on at a refinery and work there until I retired. That's what just about everyone else in our part of the country did after high school," he says.

Instead, he coached high school football until he was 34 years old, a fact which helps explain why Bum is without highfalutin airs. He came up from the bottom, slowly, to reach the top of his profession, yet he has never lost his perspective or his wit.

"There are two kinds of coaches in this business," he drawls. "Them that get fired and them that's gonna get fired."

In the 19-year history of the American Football Conference (formerly AFL), only four coaches have won more games, including playoff victories, than Bum: Don Shula (39 wins), John Madden (38), Sid Gillman (37), and Ted Marchibroda (36). Bum Phillips has won 35.

Bum has been both good and lucky. He's been pink-slipped only twice.

"I coached for 21 years and the Turk never caught me," he says with a pinch of satisfaction between his cheek and gum. "Then I was fired twice in a row, first with the San Diego Chargers and then at Southern Methodist. Change that. We really didn't get *fired* at San Diego. Sid (Gillman) kinda went up and quit for all of us."

Less than three years later, Gillman was looking for a defensive coordinator to serve under him at Houston and remembered his old defensive coordinator at San Diego. Bum accepted, and 10 months later, he became the ninth coach in the Oilers' 16-year history, and three weeks after that, he assumed Gillman's general manager duties as well.

It was Valentine's Day 1975. The change of guard was swift and not very subtle. Gone was a high-strung football coach who wore bow ties and smoked pipes. In his place was a quaint cattleman who told funny stories, drove pickup trucks, wore pointy-toed cowboy boots everywhere but to bed and chewed a plug-and-a-half of tobacco a day. Gillman was a driver; Phillips was considered a motivator. Gillman was polished; Phillips was spit. Gillman was out, Phillips in.

Gillman explained the decision to appoint a head coach from within the system in terms of himself: "I had established a good system and hired Bum to maintain it." However, Bum didn't feel obligated to The System and it became understandably easier to carry out his own programs when Gillman left Houston by mutual consent with owner Bud Adams.

Right away, a few observers of the club felt Phillips was "too soft" and the practices were "too easy" and the players would soon become spoiled country-club kids.

"There's a difference," Bum defends even today, "between bitchin' and coachin'. If you're hollerin' and wavin' your arms, that don't necessarily mean you're coachin'.

"I mean I raised six kids. The first one I whipped the daylights out of it. The second one not as much. The third one not at all. By then, I learned you can discipline a person without beatin' him."

So don't tell Bum he runs a country club. He just runs a team that players like.

"You have to be organized. But we're not a slave organization. You don't want to be so damn organized that a guy feels like a puppet on a string. You gotta have guys that got enough . . . uh, nerve or somethin' to take a chance. I don't mean gamblers. I mean guys that will take a risk as long as it's a calculated risk.

"We got a bunch of 'em on our football team. You gotta have

'em to get this far. I'd say we got 30 to 35 out of 45. We still have a few young fellas that ain't confident enough to take a risk, but that's all right."

There was mild skepticism voiced by a few coaches when the league owners approved the "16-4" scheduling format at the winter meetings in 1977. What this meant was a reduction of preseason games from six to four and an increase of regular season games from 14 to 16.

"The problem," Chuck Noll said half-kiddingly, "is that the younger teams won't have as much time to evaluate their rookies now . . . and the older teams may feel that 16 games is too long."

Then you had Bum's opinion.

"Aw heck," he drawled, "if you can't figure out in two weeks of practice and four preseason games whether some rookie's got what you're lookin' for, you ain't a coach and ain't never gonna be. And if you can't show your stuff in that time, you ain't the kind of a player any coach is gonna want."

Bum is an astute judge of football players, which is evident by his success in the free-agent market. He brings them in, looks them over and then decides their future with the Houston Oilers, if any.

"By far the toughest thing about coachin' is havin' to tell a player he can't play. Because you're not just cuttin' him; you're cuttin' his family. You're cuttin' his livelihood. And the bad part about it, most of 'em won't agree with you because human nature thinks the other guy's at fault. We all blame the other guy, although I try like hell not to ever do that. There's only one way I can progress as a coach, and that's if I put the blame on the one guy I can do something about . . . and that's me."

Bum has always been a good ol' country boy with a heart as big as a ranch's north forty. He has always liked people and talked football and that has given him self-assurance from job to job, level to level, schoolboy to professional. But even he will admit there was a "breaking in" period that all rookies experience.

"I'm not as scared as I was when I first started coachin' here," he says. "Whenever you start somethin' new, you tend to think things are a lot tougher than they probably are. Especially in the

NFL and as a head coach, because there ain't but 28 of them jobs in the world. I'm confident now that it ain't gonna be me that costs us a game. Nobody *wants* to be the guy that loses the game, whether it's the coach or the players, and that's why I don't ever blame one guy for a loss. I know I could be in the same boat. It could be me.

"I've enjoyed the division we're in. I think the AFC Central Division is a helluva division. You want to know something. It's a real honor to me to play good football teams. I don't think you prove a damn thing in football beatin' somebody that you know you oughta beat.

"But I think that's part of coachin'. The ability to keep your team progressin' all year long, that's the real key. I think the measurement of a guy's coachin' ability is not how many games he wins but how his team progresses, if he's able to keep everybody up after a tough loss and keep everybody from gettin' too high after a big win. That's the biggest thing in coachin' . . . handlin' your football team.

"A lot of people want to say football players play just for the money. Don't believe it. When the game starts, they don't have any friends. I've had guys that were brothers and they fought tooth and toenail against each other. When the opening whistle blows, those folks on the other side are your enemy."

Football is a game for the players, but it often becomes an ugly business for the coaches. Some have even awakened one morning to find "For Sale" signs planted in their front lawns when they really hadn't entertained any thought of moving. "If you're lookin' for security," Bum muses, "you sure as hell don't go into coaching."

There was a group picture taken at a meeting of NFL head coaches in the spring of 1975, at which time Bum was indoctrinated into the fraternity and was pictured sort of smiling for the camera. Twenty-six men made up the group (Seattle and Tampa Bay hadn't entered the league). Now, less than five years later, only seven of them are still employed as head coaches by the same team: Tom Landry, Bud Grant, Don Shula, Chuck Noll, Ted Marchibroda, Bart Starr and O.A. Phillips.

"I can look in the mirror every morning when I shave," Bum

says with the sincerity that has become as much of a trademark as his cowboy hats and his boots. "I mean if I know I've done everything I can do and that still ain't enough, then hell with it. But I want to make damn sure I've done everything I can do. That's one reason I haven't taken off a whole lot of time. I want to be real close by if somethin' happens."

Darrell Royal once defined Bum Phillips as "a coach's coach whose defensive innovations have spread throughout the country." Defense was his major. The "34" defense, which Oklahoma first used against Army in 1946, has become Bum's baby with the Oilers. He understands it, likes it and understands *why* he likes it.

"All your linemen in professional football got their hand on the ground," he explains, "which means they're not gonna be as quick to pursue as a guy standin' up that can see the ball real clear.

"Okay, if you got *three* linebackers standin' up that can flow quickly to the ball, they're not gonna be as effective pursuitwise as *four* guys standin' up that can flow quickly to the ball. That's one reason why I say we don't have many long runs made on us, because we got a better pursuit pattern with more people in it.

"Everybody tends to think football's somethin' hard to do. It's not hard to do. There's so damn many plays in football in which the instant they snap the football you know where they're goin'. Now the next thing is, can you get there? With three linebackers, you got three guys that recognize it real quick . . . and three guys can't chase it as well as four guys.

"Take a sweep or a quick-pitch. If you got four guys standin' up that can recognize it real quick, they got a whole lot better chance that the play ain't gonna break for any long yardage. That's the main thing with defense. Don't let 'em break the long one. If you can hold 'em to four and two and three and seven and two, pretty soon they'll bust a play or you'll throw 'em for no gain or a loss. They'll have to punt."

The "34" defense has allowed the Houston Oilers to have an active, aggressive defense that can slug it out with even the Pittsburgh Steelers and expect to win.

"We talk about pursuit all the time," Bum says. "Our guys

have got confidence now that if anyone can just get ahold of the guy with the ball — and hold on for just a second — they're gonna get plenty of help in a hurry. And they do. Then if you get a lot of pursuit, hell, it encourages you to pursue more yourself."

Bum's philosophy isn't that difficult to understand. But then, common sense never is.

Bumisms

Of course, since Bum's philosophy and common sense are one and the same, it stands to reason that most people could profit from his views on things. All kinds of things.

And Bum has been asked, or has thought, or has spoken about a lot of topics.

'Course, most of what Bum likes to talk about is football and football players. That stands to reason, too. Since he's a football coach. But a lot of things about football apply to life in general, on the sidewalks and on the streets as well as on the sidelines and on the field.

And in his folksy, friendly, and always honest way, he can put thoughts and words together so that they're fun to remember and helpful when the storm clouds gather.

Here're some of his comments, some Bumisms if you will, that are worth hangin' on to:

Good Ol' Boys Lesson
"If you gouge a guy, he'll strike back. That used to bother me when I was 40. Not anymore. If he don't strike back, he ain't worth a damn. Them good ol' boys will get you beat, 21-7."

The Back-Door Policy
"You gotta have rules, but you also gotta allow for a fella to mess up every once in awhile."

Breathing Room
"Another thing you learn after awhile is not to force a guy into makin' a decision. Because once he says 'no,' he has a hard time backin' off, whether it's a player or an owner. Next day ask him the same thing and maybe that's all he needed . . . another day."

How To Make Friends
And Influence Football Players

"Friendship is nothing you can *take* from a guy. He has to *give* it. So you got to stop and smell the flowers every now and then. I mean you got to take the first step."

A Word About Friends

"When it's the fourth quarter and your butt is draggin' and it's hot and you're gettin' beat, it's hard to give up on a friend.

Nod 'n Grin Rule

"There are people, maybe two or three, that ain't gonna like you. Not everybody likes everybody. My grandpa used to say, 'Just nod 'n grin.'

"P.S. I also learned this from Sid Gillman."

Practice Defined

"Practices are meaningful and not some place where you can sweat out all the beer you drank the night before."

Rationalization Defined

"I always thought I could coach. I just thought people were poor judges of good coaches."

High Centers

"I usually try and stay away from contract negotiations. But sometimes they get on high centers. You know, when you live in the country and you're drivin' a wagon over them old ruts, all of a sudden you're on high centers. Your wheels are spinnin' but you ain't going nowhere.

How To Fail

"Part of football is failing. Hell, if you attempt 40 tackles, you're gonna fail in 10 of 'em. If you attempt to catch 100 passes, you're gonna fail to catch 10 of 'em. A guy ain't a failure until he starts blamin' the weather or the quarterback or somebody else. As long as he puts the blame on hisself for those 10 passes he dropped, he's got a chance to drop but nine next time."

A Word About Morale
"Every team better have good morale. The team that feels like "boy, this is a great place to be," is the team that's gonna win."

Optimist's Credo
"Everybody says, 'You-all gotta play Pittsburgh twice.' I like to think, 'Pittsburgh's gotta play us twice, too.' "

A Short Essay About X's and O's
"Defense is so much easier to play than offense. It's a matter of determination and courage and just wantin' to. Defense is a guy goin' out there and reactin' to something. Offense, you've gotta plan something. It takes 11 people to put a runnin' play together. One guy can make a tackle."

Pasteurization Without Resignation
"We've had games where we had plenty of opportunities to let our milk down. If people never milked a cow, they don't understand that. Well, I have and I do. When you walk up to a cow, you can't milk her. A cow has got to let her milk down. She's gotta give it to you; you can't take it away from one. You ain't strong enough. We've had games where we could've let our milk down. In other words, we had opportunities to give up . . . but we didn't."

How To Spit Tobacco
In a Public Place

"That's easy," Bum says, "you don't."

To follow Bum's advice brings the thought to mind of his clean-shaven face turning the color of Kermit the Frog.

"Naw, I can sit through a double-feature movie and never spit. I can drive from Houston to Austin and never spit. Be a little like holdin' a cigarette in you mouth and not puffin' it. Just about that simple."

Bum packed the first pinch of chew in his cheek at the age of 14. Or was it 13? He can't be sure.

"But I do remember that it was my Grandpa Phillips that gave me my first chew," he recalls. "Well, on second thought, he may not gave it to me; I may just captured some of it."

Bum has been chewing a plug-and-a-half of White Natural Tinsley a day since 1937, which may or may not be an entry in the Guinness Book of Records.

"That's a plug-and-a-half a day, 365 days a year for 42 years," Bum calculates quickly. "I guess you could fill up a good-sized room from ceilin' to floor with what I've chewed."

White Natural Tinsley ("It don't have all that syrup and juice in it") has ranged in price over the years from 12 cents a plug to 51 cents a plug, and Bum continues to buy it by the box.

"It's the only kind I ever saw my Grandpa chew," he says. "I didn't know they made anything else."

Bum sits behind his massive (and cluttered) desk with his reptilian boots propped up on one corner and spits into anything that is convenient. An empty paper cup does fine. A trash can is easier to hit.

"Somebody gave me a solid brass spittoon once as a gift . . . but my wife, Helen, took it and planted flowers in it."

CHAPTER IX

Seven Rules For Coaching Forty-Five Large Men

He is a country philosopher who is refreshingly different in today's football society. As refreshing as the doctor who still makes house calls. Bum is an amiable soul, a trusted companion, a respected coach.

He follows a very reasonable set of seven rules and regulations.

One, Bum never scrimmages Oiler against Oiler, not even in training camp. "What for?" he asks. "Houston's not on our schedule." This avoids one of his players being maimed by a teammate.

Two, Bum seldom *drills* his players more than 65 or 75 minutes a day. "I think a guy ought to have a certain amount of repetition, but he's gotta be convinced that he's gotta get better at the repetition, not just do repetition for repetition's sake. Twelve repetitions in a two-minute period don't teach you as much as five repetitions with the thought, 'I want to do something better this time.' If you want conditioning, wait 'til practice is over and run."

Three, Bum demands extra effort. "I like effort and extra effort," he says. "If you don't like my attitude, see your friendly player rep."

Four, Bum preaches daily improvement among his players. "Be able to come away saying, 'I did *this* better today.' If he started out even with the guy he's competitin' against and improves everyday, well, three weeks from now he's better than the other guy and three months from now he's beatin' the hell out of him. A football season is like a football game; you try to be better in the fourth quarter. Most of the time, the team that progresses a little bit as the season goes is the better team."

Five, Bum always invites the players' families to Saturday practice (before a Sunday game) and lets then go home early —

together.

Six, Bum expects his players to be self-motivated, not driven. "You can't win today by embarrassin' football players," he explains. "If I played for a guy who shouted at me, I'd sock him."

Seven, Bum never solicits advice from his wife, Helen. "I don't help her cook and she don't help me coach. She's a good wife that way. Oh, lemme tell you, she don't like to lose. She ain't friendly to me when we got beat but she's understandin'. She's gotta be. Hell, I've taken one week off in 39 years. That don't exactly make me Husband of the Week."

Bum is more than a witty, well-schooled defensive football mind. He is a handler of men, all kinds of men, ranging from a former City of Houston fireman named James Young, who plays left defensive end for the Oilers, to the Austrian field-goal kicker named Toni Fritsch who speaks four languages fluently, none of them Texan.

And to think some NFL coaches still believe the way to Super Bowl XIV is by way of a chalkboard. Did common sense go out of style and nobody mentioned it?

"He Ain't No Bum."

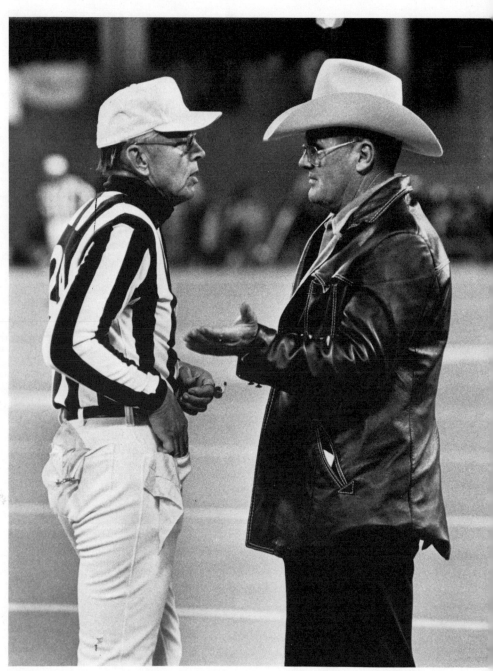

Bum gets along . . .

... with the officials ...

... most of the time.

Bum never wears his hat indoors ... even in the Astrodome.

Bum dons a tuxedo for only the third time in his life to accept the Texas Coach of the Year award from the Texas Sports Writers Association in 1975. But at least they let him wear his boots!

"I'm not too comfortable in mine either," Roger Staubach seems to be saying after being presented the 1975 Texas Pro Athlete of the Year award.

"Skoal brother?" asks Earl Campbell as his agent, Mike Trope, smiles approvingly.

Lessons learned well in July . . .

. . . mean big wins in December.

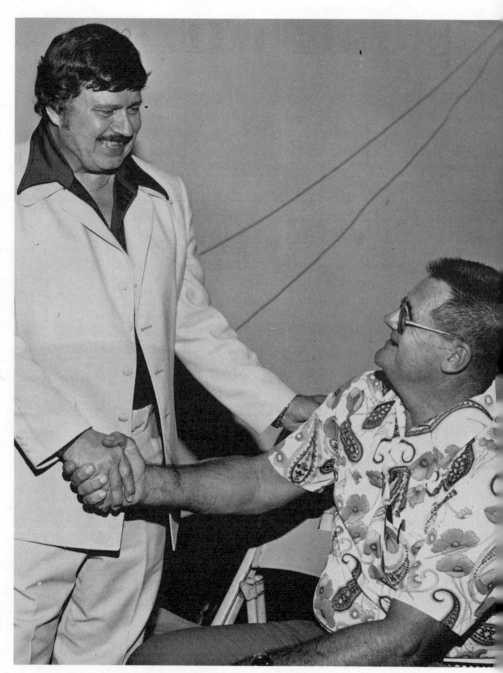

Owner Bud Adams congratulates Bum after beating the Bengals in December, 1977 to insure a winning season of 8-6.

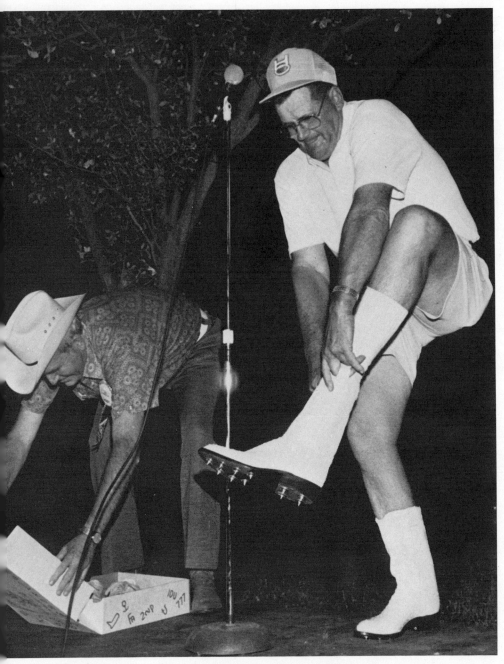

The San Angelo Chamber of Commerce presented Bum with a custom-made pair of golf boots during training camp in 1978.

Bum enjoys another victory with Carl Mauck, "the singin' Oiler."

January 7, 1979 — it was a cold and dreary day in Pittsburgh . . .

... but 50,000 die-hard fans made things warm and bright again in the Astrodome.

CHAPTER X segment

People-Watching

In his own subtle way, Bum can reveal things about people that become obvious only after he points them out. He has an uncanny knack of reducing a complex personality to a paragraph. He can expose qualities in a person that are often overlooked or taken for granted by his peers. Bum is a 20-20 people-watcher.

This is what he has to say about some of the game's leading men:

Terry Bradshaw, quarterback of the Super Bowl champion Pittsburgh Steelers: "Great leader. He's gotta be a great leader to lead that team. Take guys like Joe Greene or L.C. Greenwood. It's so much harder for *them* to respect you. You gotta be damn good. You can't be counterfeit. I don't mean this like it sounds, but you don't have to be real smart to be a good leader. You have to be yourself. You have to be *you*. Football players, who have been around so many types of people, recognize a counterfeit quicker than anything. They'd rather you be not so smart as long as you're fair.

"I'm not saying Terry Bradshaw ain't smart, because he's gotta be smart to do what he does, but the Pittsburgh players respect him because he's *him*. He ain't no put-on. He's going to be the same guy 3 o'clock in the morning as he is 3 o'clock in the afternoon. That's why they respect him. That's why he can lead 'em. He never has changed.

"Personally, I think what I like best about Terry is that he's kinda country like me. There ain't no pretense to him. He'll take a dip of snuff or wear a cowboy hat or wear boots or do whatever he wants to do. It's not that he's successful and can get by with it now. He's always been this way. That's the good part."

Don Shula, coach of the Miami Dolphins: "Now there's a great football coach, and a good man. He can take his'n and beat your'n or he can take your'n and beat his'n. I think he's the perfect example of a football coach that has the knowledge of the game and other things that go with it. There are things other than X's and O's. He's influenced a helluva lot of people to go into coaching . . . (grinning) and the SOB has influenced a lot of 'em to get out of it, too."

Jack Ham, perennial All-Pro linebacker of the Steelers: "Super football player. Don't say nothin'. Ain't a yapper or a talker; just goes out and does his job better than anybody else. He don't brag about it and he don't bitch about it. He's my kind of guy. You can't get him off his feet, and if you can, you can't *keep* him off. He's got a knack for being on the ball. I don't know if he's that great an athlete. I mean I know he's a good athlete but there are a lot of good athletes. He's a combination guy: good athlete, good coordination, good mental outlook and good feel for the game.

"And Jack Ham does something all good football players do. He has the ability to make his own mind up and take a little risk. Some players know the proper thing to do but sometimes they can't do it. He has the judgement to do what he can."

Woody Hayes, former Ohio State football coach: "He's a guy who coached too long in all probability. I'm sure I'll coach too long, too, but you hope you don't. But it gets in your blood and you believe you can coach forever. Don't get me wrong, I can't criticize Woody Hayes because he's done so much for this game. He just got a little old. He's always been a little cantankerous but just the last two or three years he got out of line sometimes. Certain age, you can't handle it and you just blow up. It's a shame."

Mean Joe Greene, perennial All-Pro defensive tackle: "He's been so good for so many years. But for awhile there, he was livin' on it rather than utilizin' it. Then one of those Pro Bowl games, he was gettin' blocked like everybody else and I think he started playin' harder. Now he's playin' like a pocketknife with two edges on it. He cuts no matter which way he goes. Ain't nothin' better than a pocketknife with two edges on it."

Art Rooney Sr., chairman of the board for the Steelers: "God, there ain't a better human being in the world than Art Rooney. I mean there ain't nobody."

Lynn Swann, Steeler wide receiver: "A tough nut. Last year, he took a lick down here in the Astrodome and they hauled him off the field at halftime. I thought they were gonna take him to the hospital, but he came back out instead and played the whole second half. He had come across the middle, and Bill Currier and

Mike Reinfeldt caught him in a high-low situation. I mean he took a terrible lick. He was hurtin' but he's a clutch player and he rises to the occasion."

Perhaps because O.A. Phillips is something right out of *The Waltons*, he affectionately refers to his players as his kids. That's right — *kids*, as in next of kin. It's natural and genuine and unabashedly Bum.

"It's not unmanly," he says, "to tell a guy you like him."

The following is a partial list of Bum's kids and how he reads them:

Dan Pastorini, quarterback: "He likes to be good. He really enjoys the big games and all the attention. But the big thing about Dan is he plays with pain, and he doesn't do it for show."

Earl Campbell, star running back and 1978 AFC Player of the Year: "It's hard to be a ceiling on how good Earl Campbell can be. He's gonna keep improvin' until he gets to the point where he don't think he can improve. Then, that's his ceiling. But right now, he's workin' like, 'God, I gotta try to make this football team.' He's such a good kid. He'll block, he'll pass protect; he'll carry the ball once or he'll carry the ball 30 times. How good can he be? How high is up?"

Billy (White Shoes) Johnson, return specialist: "They put somethin' on him that soap and water won't wash off. I mean he can move. It's hard for a bunch of 'em to touch him, let alone one. He can change the field position for you faster than anyone except the officials. When Billy goes back to return a kick, you think they're gonna play the National Anthem 'cause everyone in the stadium is on their feet."

Carl Mauck, 32-year-old veteran center: "Mauck's always bitchin'. I woke him up one morning in his hotel room and he was like an old bear. That would've worried me when I was younger. Now I'd rather he'd *say* it than get out of bed and *think* it all the way to the door. You tell Mauck what you want done and ignore his bitchin'. He'll get it done exactly the way you want it."

Tim Wilson, running back: "You never have to say a word to Tim Wilson. I mean not a word."

Gregg Bingham, inside linebacker: "Another one of them that you have to nod 'n grin at. He has his whole life programmed and he can't stand someone who doesn't. But some guys are not always on time. I know Gregg thinks I should fine 'em but I'm finin' a guy's family over a 30-second thing. Life's too short. But lemme tell you, Gregg Bingham is the guy you need. He'll play when you're 40 points ahead or 40 points behind. He's thinkin' about *today*. His career is *today*.

Willie Alexander, veteran cornerback in his ninth season with the Oilers: "Wille is a self-made football player, a *dedicated* self-made football player. He knows all the techniques, knows what to do, and he's intelligent enough to know his limitations. A lot of people aren't. Alot of people think they can outrun everybody. They can't and they find it out but it costs them first. I really don't know what Willie would run. I have no idea. I don't want to know."

(When further pressed, Bum finally estimated Alexander's time in the 40-yard dash between 4.75 and 4.9 seconds, slow by NFL cornerback standards. "But he don't get beat many times," Bum shrugged, "so I don't care.")

Ted Washington, outside linebacker and one of only 13 players left over from the pre-Bum era: "He's a guy you don't hear a whole lot about. But if you ask a tight end about Teddy Washington, he can tell you all you need to know. He is super strong, sorta like an oil drum settin' in the ground."

Mike Barber, tight end: "He has made hisself into one of the better blockin' tight ends, if not the *best* blockin' tight end in the whole league. Now the funny thing about that is when we first got him, he wanted to catch the ball and didn't care about blockin'. Now, buddy, he does it. Know why? Because he's one of them guys that when he found out the *team* needed him to be a good blocker, he did it. They must not have tried to convince him of that at Louisiana Tech."

Kenny Burrough, wide receiver: "Ah, gol-lee, you can talk a week about Kenny Burrough. He's in a class all by hisself. He's a guy that can outrun anybody I've ever seen. He's a great athlete and then a super kid to go along with it. Great team man. He'll play a ball game and sometime never catch a pass, but it don't upset him one bit. He ain't like a lot of prima donnas. Kenny Burrough's not a prima donna; he's a team man. He takes those long, smooth strides. You look up and he's four yards from ya; you bat your eyes and he's four yards beyond ya. When Kenny starts to move, he goes straight into overdrive. The people here don't appreciate him like they should."

Watching
The People-Watcher

If Bum is a 20-20 people-watcher, he has a lot of eyes looking his way, too.

His down-to-earth ways have been duly noted by a host of people in pro football. And they have some comments about Bum Phillips as a human being and as a coach. Here are some samples of what kind of reaction he gets:

Terry Bradshaw,
quarterback of the Pittsburgh Steelers:

"Bum Phillips is a guy I'm just naturally drawn to because of his personality, his warmth, his friendliness, his honesty. I mean he's so doggone sincere. I love him. It's like a father-son relationship, even though I play for probably the Oilers' biggest rival.

"He's the kind of guy you'd go to war for, fight for, give your life for. I have the utmost respect for him. I'm crazy about the guy. He's a super human being. It's nice to know there are coaches in our business who love their players. He can get more out of them without hollering than anybody I've ever seen. It would be very easy to get up and play for him.

"I keep in touch with him during the off-season. I'll call him up and we'll talk about horses. Bum Phillips is a friend of mine. He's a very special person to me. I hope we will always remain friends, wherever I go."

Joe Greene,
Steelers defensive tackle:

"Most of all I think of him as an honest man. He seems to enjoy what he's doing. I think he really likes football, I get that impression. I get the impression he is a highly competitive but he knows how to lose.

"He's made comments about Pittsburgh when we played him; comments that no one else does. Most coaches say, 'Blah, blah . . . we have to do our best.' Bum doesn't give you all that bull. He calls it like it is. Reporters must like to talk to him; I like to listen to him.

"He wants to be real. I think it would really hurt if he came off as a plastic person.

"I'm from Texas. I look on him as an individual. That's a problem a lot of us have with our profession; we aren't what we think we are. Some guys on our team; I know it's true with me, too. I find myself trying to be something I really *am*. At this point in time, I play football and I'm damn proud of it. I respect the man for being what he is. That's all you can ask."

Sid Gillman,
special assistant to the Philadelphia Eagles:

"When I went to the San Diego Chargers, I needed somebody to coordinate my defense. Actually, I wanted somebody from college football because college football coaches can drill people; that's what football is all about, especially among the assistants. So, I called all my friends around the colleges; Bear Bryant was one of them. I wanted to know who was a good drillmaster. Bear recommended Bum Phillips and that was good enough for me. I've never been sorry for it. He is a fine drillmaster and knows defenses as well as anybody.

"When I left the Chargers, Bum coached at Oklahoma State and Texas A&M, then when I got the Houston job I naturally called upon Bum again. Of course, Bum joined me. Then when I decided I wouldn't coach the Houston Oilers anymore, I immediately thought of Bum as my successor. What our system needed was continuity, which he could give.

"He's typically Texas. He fits the job. To know Bum Phillips is to love him. He has great football knowledge. He has been a success and will always be a success. The cowboy hat and Bum Phillips fit. A chaw of tobacco fits. All he needs is a holster. Anybody that knows Bum Phillips can't feel that he's putting on a show. If he was running a beauty parlor, he would wear boots and a cowboy hat and spit tobacco. There was nobody else left on the list after the great Bear said Bum could do the job. When he got off the airplane that day, I was waiting for him at the airport. Thirty or 130 people got off, it didn't matter. I could pick him out. I just knew that was Bum Phillips."

Billy Sullivan,
president of New England Patriots:
"If he says he thinks the world of me, I can't think of a nicer compliment I could receive. I think he is the most refreshing person — I'd like to say character, but sometimes people refer to that as a clown — but I think he is the most refreshing personality to come into National Football League during my lifetime.

"I had a chance to see it first hand, during the playoffs, where he never thought once to promote Bum Phillips. He's a totally unselfish man. He is a complete success of a human being. I might implement that winning the Super Bowl is the epitome of our business, and so being a Super Bowl person might be a better person, but I've never met anyone that enhanced the stature of our profession better than this man.

"To give you an example: I played golf with him recently and afterwards asked him to have a drink with me. He said, 'I'm sorry but I have to leave because I have to do something important.' Well, just before leaving he finally admitted that he was driving to Beaumont, Texas, 90 miles away, to attend a testimonial dinner for his high school football coach. In his pickup truck! You know he drives a pickup truck, and in back of it he has two boxes. One contains 500 gallons of gasoline that he loads up in August to carry him through the football season, and in the other box he has his fishing gear and golf clubs.

"I think he would be just as happy coaching a high school team. I think he recognizes that he has a way with men, a way to get them to do things. He's the most refreshing breeze that has ever blown into the NFL. A football team is nothing more than an extension of the coach. No one can more rally men around him more than Bum, because he has battled the odds all his life. He has lived in anonymity.

"There isn't a more dominant personality today on any level of coaching than Bum Phillips. Let me say, you're writing about a guy who is almost a saint in our business. I don't think this guy even knows how to lie."

Louie Kelcher,
San Diego defensive tackle:

"He is really a player's coach. He was our defensive coordinator at SMU in my sophomore year. An easy man to understand. Coaching is not a popularity contest, but most players that play for him like him.

"The first time I met him, I knew this guy meant business. Even though he had a crewcut, a chaw of tobacco and talked country, I knew he knew what he was talking about. He worked the jokes in with the business. When Hayden Fry (then head coach at SMU) got fired, the majority of the players wanted Bum to stay as head coach, that's how much they thought of him. It was an awkward situation for Bum, so he left.

"I played for him just one year, but that one year has helped me tremendously in my career. I was pretty raw as a sophomore in college. Bum showed me how to do things and helped me mature a little at the same time. When he tells you something, you automatically want to do it for him."

CHAPTER XII

It's Human Nature

It's human nature to be liked. Bum's no exception to that. And he also likes people. People from everywhere, who do most anything and everything. And he's just as big a hero-worshipper as anyone.

Muhammad Ali stopped by an Oilers practice one afternoon early in the 1979 season. The champ's visit was unannounced.

Bum was chatting with some visitors after practice. All of a sudden he broke the conversation and jumped to his feet. "Hey, I wanna meet that man," he said.

The visitors looked to see where Bum was headed. They did a double-take when they also saw Ali amid some of the Oilers.

When Bum reached the cluster, he just stood back, takin' in the scene. Then someone introduced him to the former heavyweight king.

"Hi champ," was Bum's greeting. He extended his hand. Ali slipped into a boxing pose, and asked, "Did you call me tramp?"

When the laughter subsided, Ali retorted, "Hey, you don't look like no Bum to me."

Visitors, with big names and little names, are frequent at Oiler practices. But not as much as in Bum's first couple of years. His invitations to come to practices simply got out of hand. Sometimes, on a Saturday morning, there were as many as 500 Little League football players showing up.

"I didn't like stoppin' all those youngsters from comin'," Bum explained. "It was good for football. It gave them a chance to see the players up close, and afterwards they could get autographs and pictures. But, heck, it got to the point that there were too many, and no way of controllin' things."

Players' families, of course, are still welcome to the Saturday sessions, and it's a real sight. Wives, kids, babies in strollers, and even the players' pet dogs line the sidelines.

Visiting media from out of town are astounded. And they naturally ask questions. And Bum naturally has answers.

"Look," explains Bum, "we take the players away from their families a whole lot. They're away at training camp most all of

July and August. Then in the season we're on the road for eight
weekends. And the players stay Saturday nights at a motel when
we're in town. That's a lot of time that Dad is away from home.
So on Saturdays, everyone has a chance to come visit Dad at
'work' and the wives get a chance to know each other. They're
part of the team, too, you know, a damn important part."

It's Bum's way of doing things, but he is quick to say that
what is his way, and what works for him, may not work for
somebody else's team.

"It don't necessarily mean our way is the only way," he says.
"We just know that our way works for us. You know, we spend
just as much time each year evaluating what kind of people are
available in the draft as we do what kind of football player they
are.

"Our whole staff goes on the road early each spring and personally visits with the guys we think most highly of as players.
Then we come back and sit down to see if those players are the
kind of people we want on our team. There's no way you can
judge a player's character on film. You have to do that face to
face, and you have to have a coaching staff who can evaluate
character, too. Not everyone can do that. And, I'm gonna tell you
now that we have been damn successful in selecting people with
character. I mean that as a tribute to our assistant coaches, and I
mean it as a tribute to the people who we have drafted and their
mommies and daddies who raised them."

Bum brags on his players, the people he works for, and the
people who work for him. And they brag on Bum.

But, it's not all a bed of roses, being so close with all of the
players. The day that Bum has to make the decision to let a player
go is the day he dreads most. Take the day just before the season
when Bum released veteran linebacker Steve Kiner:

"I hated it, always have, and always will. It's the worst part
of football," Bum says. "You're telling him that he can't play for
you anymore. You're firing him from his job, and you're taking
his livelihood away from him. With Steve, it hurt even worse
because here was a guy who never in five years missed a game,
never missed a practice. Heck, he wasn't even late for a meeting.
He was the perfect team-player. He did anything we ever asked

of him, played special teams, everything. But, we had to decide whether to keep Steve or a younger player. And our decision, right or wrong, was to go with the younger player. That didn't make telling Steve any easier. And I know that Steve felt it was the end of the world.

"But I don't mind tellin' anyone that football isn't everything in life. Sometimes us coaches or the players think it is, and sometimes us in football have presented that image. Mistakenly so, in my opinion. But believe me, it's not. And, anyone who thinks so ought to take a walk through Texas Children's Hospital sometime. That'll change your outlook in a hurry on what's important and what isn't."

Before Bum ever led the Oilers on the field for a game as a head coach, veteran Tommy Maxwell, the first player Bum cut in his first season, must have known what was ahead.

Packing his bags at training camp in Huntsville on a July afternoon in 1975, Maxwell told reporters: "You know, I only have one regret in football. And that is I never had the chance to play for that man. I would have enjoyed that."

It's just human nature to want to play for Bum. Veteran all-pro Elvin Bethea chided the media at that 1975 training camp. He got tired of reading all the stories being written about how relaxed the Oiler training camp was under the first-year coach. And how happy all of the players were. "Hey, you guys," Bethea said at dinner one evening, "cut out them kind of stories. If that word gets around to the other camps, a lot of great players are gonna play out their options to come here, and then a lot of us are gonna be out of jobs here."

Bum says, "Nobody works *for* me. They work *with* me, and I work *with* them."

That's Bum putting human nature to work. And for Bum, it works.

The Stoic Quarterback

They often meet over barbecued ribs and cold beer in an out-of-the-way bar-and-grill called the Swinging Door near Bum's horse barns in Missouri City, just the two of them. The Coach and The Quarterback, the decision-maker and the spear-carrier.

This one particular time, Dan Pastorini brought a date and found Bum working on his third can of Coors in the rear of the establishment. Another round of ribs, please. A beer for the gentleman and the lady. Good times. Bum should have been a social director.

Finally, they discussed the goal-line offense they planned to use against the Cincinnati Bengals in less than 48 hours. Pastorini's date listened politely. She must have been wondering how many coaches in the National Football League have barbecue sauce instead of chalk dust on their fingers as they discuss strategy with their quarterbacks.

Bum and Dan enjoy a relationship closer than coach and player. Pastorini likes Bum's honesty and openness; Bum admires his quarterback's ability and courage.

"You want a guy who ain't afraid to play with a little pain," Bum says. "I don't mean an injury; there's a difference. An injury you don't play with. But what if you have a headache? You play. Well, a sprained ankle is no different than a headache. You tape it and play.

"Terry (Bradshaw) and Dan are alike that way. Both these kids will play, I don't care what's wrong with 'em. They play whether they got a broken wrist or a broken rib, and the other players respect them for that.

"People assume the quarterback is automatically a leader, but he's not. Leadership isn't something that somebody can hand you like a position you play. It don't automatically go with the job. Dan had to earn it, and he did.

"There wasn't a better team man than John Hadl. Well, Dan is gonna be just like that in two or three years. He cares about this team. Nobody knows how much he does care. Dan doesn't even know it. But you can see it happenin'. He's gonna be just like

Hadl . . . and I've said it many times, if you don't like John Hadl you don't like me.

"When I worked for Bear Bryant (1957) at Texas A&M, it didn't make no difference who made a mistake, Bear would always say, 'I caused it.' If a guy really has confidence in hisself, he ain't afraid to take the blame. Bryant was that way. Hadl was that way. In fact, Dan is already startin' to get that way. He volunteers it even if it isn't his fault."

Bum is bullish on camaraderie. He regrets there aren't more parties for his players.

"There are times when Dan will take a group of 'em out and drink some beer, maybe the linebackers one time and the defensive backs another. The Oilers pay for it. They have a few beers and then everybody goes home. Morale and pullin' together, it's a helluva lot more important in football than in the oil business."

Pastorini is a poised and thoughtful leader, but he doesn't always do what is best for his body. He has a tendency to be more competitive than cautious, which was evident in the Oilers' 27-10 victory over Pittsburgh in '77. Instead of grounding the football or throwing an incompletion, Pastorini tried to outmaneuver Mean Joe Greene and ended up with a severely sprained ankle and mildly aching back instead.

"Dan didn't have to get hurt," Bum said. "He got hurt because he's a competitor. He thinks every time he throws a football, he's gonna throw it for a touchdown. He wants to complete everything he throws and he *thinks* he's gonna complete everything he throws."

There was a time during the '77 season that the casualty list among NFL quarterbacks was escalating at the alarming rate of the no-show fans in Buffalo. The AFC Central was hit hard. Terry Bradshaw wore a flexible cast on his left wrist, Ken Anderson limped with a strained left knee and a bruised right thigh, and Pastorini had a plastic cast of his own on his right ankle. Brian Sipe kept looking over his shoulder and left his house only when necessary.

Bum made a couple of pithy comments about the state of the AFC Central at the time. On Bill Johnson, a good buddy from Texas and then-coach of the Cincinnati Bengals: "I don't think he can get outcoached; I do think he can get outinjured." On the Oilers' chances in the very competitive AFC Central: "It's a dog-fight. I just hope we can fight, and we're not the dogs."

Well, Pastorini really came of age that '77 season. He took charge. He took it upon himself to become a leader, not just a quarterback.

Bum saw it coming. "He did something he never did before. He came down all during the off-season and worked out with our offensive linemen. I mean he got in there and worked every drill with 'em. He prepared hisself better than I ever seen a quarter-back prepare. He worked harder than anybody we had. He'd do all his own drills and then he'd go work out with the offensive linemen and do some more."

Nearly eighty per cent of the Oilers live in the Houston area during the off-season, and they would meet on their own at 1 p.m., in the heat of the day and sweat together.

"That damn Dan was out there everyday, workin' like the devil," Bum recalled those months leading up to the '77 season. "And he had something he never had before. He had the respect of all of the other football players because he was out there everyday, all day long, doing what they were doin'. It's kinda hard to ask somebody to do something unless they feel like you're willin' to do the same thing.

Pastorini could've been another Ray Guy, according to Bum. "If he just punted and that's all he had to do, he'd be the best. He really has a natural kicking style. It's just as straight as can be; he don't swing across the body."

Pastorini has punted for the Oilers in the past but has become too valuable as a quarterback to pull double-duty. It just isn't worth the risk of injury.

"He's a good athlete," Bum will tell you. "For a guy who can't run, he's a helluva athlete. The Lord didn't make him fast. He's coordinated well, except for that coordination of putting one foot in front of the other. It isn't fast enough."

Interestingly, Bum was never a burner in his playing days. In fact, to this day, he loathes any form of running.

"Now Dan has his little temper tantrums," Bum continues. "People say we don't have discipline, but you don't win in the clutch if you don't have discipline. I learned you can discipline a person without beatin' him."

Pastorini has a stubborn streak (not unlike Bum) that has a tendency to jeopardize the working parts of his body. He won't sit down unless he's placed in traction. He won't miss a game unless he's confined to intensive care. He won't admit to having an incapacitating injury until they administer Last Rights.

A classic example of his stoicism was the second Steeler game of the '77 season. Pastorini was still maimed from the first Steeler confrontation two weeks earlier. This time the site was Three Rivers Stadium and the sight was often gory.

"We shouldn't have played Dan," Bum recalls. "We played him partly because of his insistence. Like I said before, Dan is a great competitor. He said, 'Shoot it, I can play.' We had a plastic cast made for his foot that supported his ankle, and the doctors assured me that he couldn't hurt it any worse.

"Of course, he wanted to play and you wanted to believe him when he said, 'I can do it.' But, really, he couldn't. He had no mobility at all. It was hard for him to take one step sideways on that ankle. Dan is not a graceful runner, but he does move away from people and get away from people. In that ball game, he couldn't.

"Against Pittsburgh, you better be able to move. When it comes time to throw the football, they can rush the passer. They're too aggressive as pass rushers to allow 'em to zero in on Dan like that. Dan was like a sittin' duck back there. They knew it and that was even worse. They knew he couldn't run out of the pocket, whereas before we could run a bootleg or what we used to call a 'waggle' or a sprintout. Now they knew if it was a passin' down, he had to throw it from seven yards straight back . . . and boy, they came a-hummin'."

Final score: Pittsburgh 27, Houston 10.

The following week, Hadl started the game against Cincinnati and couldn't move the offense. Bum had decided to hog-tie Pastorini to the bench, and he stuck with that decision until the Oilers were faced with losing, 10-0, midway through the third quarter. Then before you could say Charlie Hennigan (three times All-Pro Oiler), there was Pastorini pitching the Oilers to a

10-10 tie and sudden-death overtime.

"Dan wasn't gonna have it any other way," Bum remembers. "Sure enough, he was right and I was wrong."

Actually, Pastorini was a quarterback with limited mileage. The team physician had informed Bum during the week, "If you're going to play Pastorini, pick your half. All he can go is about 1½ quarters."

Bum stayed with Hadl until it was Cincinnati 10, Houston 0, and the balding backup quarterback had completed only five passes for 17 yards and one interception. It was Pastorini time. The stoic quarterback, who had agonized for more than three quarters on the Oiler sidelines, took the field and directed them on two scoring drives.

Because Earl Campbell was still playing for the Texas Longhorns, Pastorini threw a quick bomb to Ken Burrough, which resulted in a 47-yard pass interference penalty against Marvin Cobb of the Bengals and led to a 22-yard field goal by Toni Fritsch.

Moments later, Pastorini marched the Oilers 73 yards in 17 plays with Ronnie Coleman taking a three-yard pass all alone in the end zone. Fritsch converted. It was 10-10.

Then came the controversial call that made line judge Vince Jacob a household word in Houston. Situation: Twenty-seven ticks on the clock. Bum decides to have Fritsch kick away, rather than onside, and the ball carries end-over-end to the goal line, near the out-of-bounds stripe on the left side, where suddenly the bouncing football and Cincinnati return man Willie Shelby avoid each other like oil and water. The football rolls free. Houston's Steve Baumgartner falls on it in the end zone.

Oiler touchdown?

Nope. Touchback, Bengals' ball on the 20.

Jacob, who was right on the play, ruled that Shelby set a touchdown-saving foot on the out of bounds stripe in the end zone as the ball came up and touched him. That's the story Bum was given. Later, Shelby, who will be remembered for his honesty and not his wisdom, admitted, "I didn't touch the ball, I know that . . . uh, why? Was I supposed to have touched it?"

Later, somebody asked Bum why he didn't try an onside kick

with 27 seconds left. "As it turned out," he drawled, "we had one helluva onside kick."

However, the game moved into overtime and the Oilers lost the coin toss. Pastorini called tails. The Bengals received the kickoff and moved into field goal range where, on second down, Chris Bahr drilled a 22-yarder that left Bum feeling as if he had just swallowed a plug of tobacco.

"If I had my choice," he offered as a bit of constructive critic ism, "I'd like to see *fulltime* officials. If they can cost me my job, I'd like to be able to cost 'em theirs. I'd like 'em to have a little more responsibility. Right now, they can go back to their insurance businesses. I really don't have an insurance business to go back to."

The Shelby misplay occurred on the Oilers' side of the field, giving Bum an excellent view. But then he assumed Jacob had a good shot of it, too.

"In the first place," Bum maintains to this day, "Shelby wasn't out of bounds. That was No. 1. The official felt like he was right and I felt like I was right. No, I *knew* I was right; he *felt* like he was right. But he ended up with the authority."

The Oilers finished 8-6 that season and Bum still can't help but think of Vince Jacob and Willie Shelby every now and then. "We thought we were 9-5," he says, "but I have had a little hell convincin' my owner of that."

Despite the fact that a television camera in the end zone would've in all probability disproved Jacob's call, Bum is opposed to instant replays for the use of officiating. "I like to see things," he explains, "settled on the field."

Bum is extremely understanding of officials, even those who blow calls that go against Houston Oilers, Inc., and can even be downright sympathetic toward them.

"The hardest damn thing in football is officiatin'," he admits. "It's even harder than playin' or coachin'. I don't care how many they call. If they call one wrong, they're wrong in front of 60,000 people. Now these instant replays (provided for television audiences) have focused so much pressure on the officials that I really feel sorry for 'em. I don't want to cause problems for 'em; they got enough problems."

However, Bum would like to see something done to eliminate sudden-death overtime in the NFL.

"It's one of them rules I think we need to change," he says very emphatically. "It doesn't seem fair that by winnin' a coin flip, a guy can win a football game. The other team don't get a chance to score. To me, you ought'n never to lose a football game without gettin' an opportunity to win it. Both teams should be allowed one possession."

Instead, Pastorini was done for the day as soon as that coin hit the AstroTurf at Riverfront Stadium.

"To get beat the way we got beat was really a helpless feelin'," Bum remembers. "I couldn't even justify bitchin' about it . . . without makin' it hard on officials. Believe me, they got a tough job. Gawdalmighty, they got a tough job."

The Renaissance Man

When Bum joined Sid Gillman's coaching staff in 1974, Earl Campbell was just graduating from Tyler (Texas) High School. In the meantime, the Houston Oilers would have to improvise. In those early years before Campbell, also known as BC, the Oilers' best chance of scoring a touchdown was a 47-yard touchdown pass from Dan Pastorini to Kenny Burrough.

It was terribly one-dimensional, a low-percentage path to the end zone. It was a little like playing poker with your cards showing. Opposing teams would practice all week on their anti-bomb defense. Bum, a lifetime student of defensive football, quickly recognized the major shortcoming of his offense: no legs.

"We didn't have a runnin' attack down here my first four years with the Oilers — one as an assistant and three as a head coach. Oh, we had some games where some people made some yards but nothin' you could hang your hat on. You go back and look at all the teams that win the Super Bowls and teams that get in the playoffs. They've got good runnin' attacks. I don't mean *sometime* runnin' attacks; I mean *consistent* runnin' attacks.

"In order to keep your defense off the field, you have to develop a runnin' attack. If you throw three (passes) and punt, you haven't really taken but 26 seconds off the clock. If you throw three incompletions, that means the other team gets the football one more time and your defense didn't get much of a chance to rest."

Completing a pass is particularly difficult when the opposition *knows* you have to throw the football. It becomes even more improbable when you're close to the goal line. Suddenly there isn't enough room to run the route. So Pastorini and Burrough liked to throw the bomb from their own end of the field. It was called "deep breath" football.

"An over-the-head catch is the most difficult catch in football," Bum observes. "It's worse than a divin' catch; it's worse than any other kind, especially when the ball is spinnin' in the air about 55 yards. It's hard to judge a ball thrown that far, period, much less comin' straight over your head. Your body ain't made so you can turn your head straight back to locate the football, but that's the way the ball comes in and that's the way you gotta do it. You can't turn your neck and watch it. You gotta look straight back and you got that helmet and that face mask and everythin' else."

Yet, Kenny Burrough has probably made more of these double-jointed, over-the-head, acrobatic catches in his 10-year NFL career than any other receiver in the game today. His 26 touchdown receptions since joining the Oilers in 1971 have averaged more than 50 yards per catch.

"The NFL doesn't keep records on that category," Bum regrets, "but we've claimed this one for Kenny. Nobody disputes it, so I'm sure it's an NFL record."

Even though Pastorini has always had plenty of arm to heave a football 50 or 60 yards in the air, a Pastorini-to-Burrough "bomb" has often come on a ball thrown about 10 yards . . . laterally. It's a slip-screen pass, in which Burrough drives off the line, stops and returns to his original start position. Pastorini fakes the run, looks deep, then spins and lays the football off to Double-0. Burrough does the rest.

"What we like to do on that pass play is get eight to 10 yards between the cornerback and Kenny," Bum says. That's usually the distance Burrough needs to make a fool out of one-on-one coverage.

Burrough came out of Texas Southern and was chosen in the first round of the '70 college draft by the New Orleans Saints. A year later, the Oilers acquired him along with defensive tackle Dave Rowe for Hoyle Granger, Terry Stoepel, Charlie Blossom and a second-round draft pick.

"What a trade that was," Bum has grown to appreciate. Actually, it was almost as great a deal as the one that put Earl Campbell's thunder in an azure-and-white Houston Oiler uniform when the Tampa Bay Bucs accepted first-year tight end Jimmy Giles and three draft choices (second, third and fifth rounds) in exchange for the No. 1 draft rights to the Tyler Rose.

"Like so many other things that happen in football, that trade worked out in a rather strange fashion. Now I sure as hell ain't any smarter than any other coach who watched Earl Campbell

play at Texas. He was a real player, a real one, and like everybody else I wanted him, but realistically there wasn't much
chance for us to get him, and I knew it. The price that Tampa Bay
would want for draft rights to him had to be too much, and it
don't help much to hurt yourself in several places just to solve
another problem," Bum maintained.

"Anyway, I met his agent on the plane back from the Senior
Bowl that January and he asked me if I wanted Earl. I gave him
the obvious answer and he told me that Earl really wanted to stay
in Texas. Well, the story of that conversation got out to a national
paper and rumors started flyin' that we were makin' a deal for
Earl. Pat Peppler, our assistant general manager, told the Tampa
people that number one, we were interested and, number two,
make the best deal they could but to give us the last shot at
maybe betterin' it.

"They said they would. Now that was back in February and,
remember, we didn't make the deal 'til April. Tampa Bay was in
the market for a quarterback and there was no way we were
gonna give up Dan, so it appeared there wasn't gonna be any deal.
We really thought Cincinnati was gonna get him. They had four
draft picks in the first two rounds that year and a backup quarterback they could deal in John Reaves, who just happened to be a
Florida boy. I thought they might put together too good a package
for anybody to better.

"Then in mid-April, the stories started flyin' that LA was
gonna make a deal for Earl's rights by trading a tight end to
Tampa Bay, along with some draft picks. Jack Cherry, our former
PR director, stopped by the office one morning and inquired
about what I thought Tampa Bay was gonna do.Out of curiosity, I
had my secretary, Dania Fisher, get John McKay on the
telephone.

"We talked for awhile and John said that he'd make a deal
with me if I'd give him Jimmy Giles, our first-round draft pick
that year, our second that year and a third the following year. I
told him 'yes' right on the spot, and he said he'd call his owner to
get the okay and call me back the next day. Well, I got off the
phone and Pat Peppler, Jack Cherry and I stood around, looked at
each other, and wondered if we were dreamin'.

"Now don't get me wrong. I'm not sayin' this as critical of
Coach McKay. The amazement on our part was that the deal he
was askin' for was not as much as I thought it would be, or anyone else for that matter. I knew they were gettin' a helluva football player in Jimmy Giles . . . but we were gettin' a helluva football player, too. You know you can hand Earl Campbell the football 25 or 30 times a game; you can get it to that second tight end
maybe twice.

"The next day came and went, without a call from Coach
McKay, and we all felt that the deal was probably off, or that Coach
McKay was shoppin' our offer around. It turned out that he *had*
called, but the telephone lines into Pat and my office were busy
so he left word with one of the switchboard girls. That was on a
Friday. She didn't give us the message until Monday morning.

"Just imagine," Bum paled, "Coach McKay could've assumed
we weren't interested anymore by not returnin' his call. So as
soon as I got the message on Monday, I called and he said we had
a deal . . . under one condition. I held my breath. He also wanted
a fifth-round pick the next year. I told him he had it and the deal
was teletyped to the league office.

"Sometimes making a trade is a very complex thing and
other times they work out simply. This turned out to be one of
the simple ones. Jack Cherry called a press conference right away
and we announced it. I don't think the City of Houston has been
the same since."

Soon reporters were probing Bum as to how Campbell would
be used, when Campbell would be used, where Campbell would
be used and how long will it take the Heisman Trophy winner to
make a significant contribution to the Houston Oilers?

"Oh, a day . . . maybe two," Bum chuckled.

Will he play fullback or halfback?

"It don't matter much where he's comin' from," Bum replied.
"It's where he's gonna go that counts."

How good can Earl Campbell be in the NFL?

"How high is up?" Bum smiled.

Have you noticed how slowly he gets up after being tackled?

"Yep," Bum responded, "but then I notice he goes down
slow, too."

Furman Bisher, sports editor of the *Atlanta Journal,* asked if Bum didn't feel a great deal of pressure coaching an Earl Campbell, and Bum thought about that for a moment before answering the question: "No, but I sure would've felt it coachin' *against* him."

The Earl Campbell questions went on and on.

What would he have been like 20 years ago?

"Ah, we would've tackled him," Bum mused, "but it would've took a lot more of us."

Can Campbell do for Houston what Tony Dorsett has done for Dallas? Twice in two years? Twice in the same state? Bum can't (and won't) make any predictions.

"But I think one runnin' back can make a football team great quicker than anythin' else other than a quarterback," he will allow. "It's hard to measure on Dallas' team because Dallas had a good football team prior to the time they got Dorsett . . . but he doggone sure didn't hurt 'em. A good runner kinda opens up other things, 'cause you got to respect him."

Campbell, as a rookie, led the NFL in rushing with 1,450 yards. He carried the football 302 times for a 4.8-yard average and 13 touchdowns. What does he do for an encore?

"Earl may be better this year than he was last year and not gain as many yards," Bum points out. "It's very simple. You can stop anybody, I don't care who it is. You can stop Earl Campbell. You can stop Franco Harris. But you may get killed with somethin' else. Look at our Miami game in the playoffs."

Indeed, the Dolphins, remembering that Campbell had embarrassed them with 199 yards rushing and four touchdowns in an earlier meeting during the '78 season, concentrated on holding him to only 16 yards on 13 carries in the first half of the AFC wildcard game Christmas Eve. However, Dan Pastorini completed 16 of 21 passes over a stacked-up Miami defense for 261 yards, en route to a 20-for-29 afternoon for 306 yards and a touchdown.

Campbell was held to 84 yards on 26 carries but the Oilers prevailed, 17-9. One-dimensional football was gone in Houston. Bum saw to that when he telephoned John McKay. When Earl reported to training camp this summer, he was four pounds heavier, one inch trimmer around the waist, had the same sized bulbous thighs and was able to accelerate the first 10 yards in 1.5 seconds.

Bum now has a running attack to hang his hat on.

No Way You Can Practice Bein' Miserable

To this day, Bum will never forget his first Monday Night red face on ABC-TV. It was 1975. The Pittsburgh Steelers came into the Astrodome and embarrassed the Oilers in front of their families, their friends and a few million other people, 32-9. "I remember Franco Harris havin' a great night," Bum regretfully recalls. "That might've been the night I made up my mind that in this league I wanted a back like him. I wanted those *other* coaches to have to face that.

"Franco has made more yards against us where he wasn't supposed to go than he has where he is supposed to go. That's a tribute to him as the kind of back he is. Some of the biggest plays he's made is when we have completely stopped the hole designed for him and he bounces out and goes around end or off tackle or reverses his field."

Unknown to him at the time, Bum was dreaming about Earl Campbell.

But Bum didn't have Earl Campbell when he took the Oiler coaching job in 1975, although he made the most of what he had and finished a surprisingly strong 10-4. The Oilers lost twice each to Pittsburgh and Cincinnati, and just missed the AFC playoffs.

"We had a lot of luck that year," Bum admits. "By lucky I mean we won all the close games. We won a close one against Oakland (27-26), against New England (7-0), against Miami (20-19), and against Washington (13-10), so we could've just as easily been 7-7. But, as it turned out, us and Miami became the first teams in NFL history to finish 10-4 and not make the playoffs.

"Washington had a heckuva club that year, and I remember it as the game the Houston fans came alive. You know, it's awful easy to get so comfortable in the Dome that you don't do much cheerin'. Well, Robert Brazile was a rookie that year and he was thrown out of the game for hittin' Billy Kilmer above the shoulders on a run. It was a rule and the official was right; it was a rookie mistake on Robert's part. But we had a sellout crowd that day and they nearly blew the roof off when Robert got thrown out for what appeared to be a clean hit. It woke up our players. We played some awful tough defense and went on to win the game."

Another vivid image that Bum has of that first season is Ronnie Coleman's seven-yard run for the winning touchdown in the final minute against Miami. "That was as great a seven-yard run as any back ever made," Bum claims. "Carl Mauck even gave him an assist to make sure he got into the end zone. Earlier Billy Johnson gave us a big lift with a punt return for a touchdown and we just kept crawlin' back on 'em. I remember Bubba Smith just joined us and blocked two extra-points in the game, and that really won it for us.

"I guess the first team that any coach has, on any level, is and will always be close to his heart. That '75 team will always have a special place in my heart. It was really Bubba Smith's last year of football, and I have known Bubba since he was a toddler in Beaumont. I knew his daddy, who coached high school ball over there, even longer. Bubba's brother, Tody, played only one more season after '75, and Freddie Willis played only another year. There were a lot of fine people on that team that aren't playin' today: Zeke Moore, who had a heckuva fine career; Fred Hoaglin, and Lynn Dickey who we traded that winter. Lynn is one of the nicest people you ever want to meet. If he hadn't had so many injuries, and I mean bad ones, he would've been a great one. I hope he comes back with Green Bay this year, because Lynn Dickey deserves some good things in football."

The Oilers deserved a better fate themselves in '76 when they slipped to 5-9. "I don't wanna remember much about that year," Bum says. "Nothin' much good happened to us. We had injuries like I've never seen before. We signed a fine safety in Mike Weger and lost him early in the year with a knee. We didn't have a first or a third or a fifth pick in the draft that year, and our second pick, Mike Barber, played only one game before havin' knee surgery. We made the mistake of tradin' away our fourth pick, Steve Largent, and lost our sixth pick, Art Stringer, when he went down in camp. We were gettin' old; we didn't have any young replacements in the draft, and now we were gettin' crippled up. Dan missed two or three games; people were keyin' on Kenny Burrough and Billy Johnson and Ronnie Coleman, and we just didn't have any firepower on offense. Our defense played like they always do, but you can't have 'em on the field all the time.

"We started off the season well and, in our fourth game, we had a chance to tie for the division lead with Cincinnati. We were playin' at San Diego and leadin' in the ball game, then all of a sudden the roof fell in. Teddy Washington went down. Billy Johnson went down. Greg Sampson went down. San Diego was runnin' the ball down our throat 'cause we had three linebackers out of the game. The next week, we came home to play Cincinnati with a patched-up team, and they blew us out. We didn't have much left, but we played all the rest of 'em, and I mean we played hard football with a lot of heart.

"I'll tell you what. About midway through the season, we went up to Cincinnati and, really, we didn't have a prayer. They were goin' good; they were healthy, and we didn't have Dan Pastorini. John Hadl did a great job pickin' them apart; Billy J. made some great catches, and damn if we don't have a 27-24 lead on 'em with less than a minute to go. On third-and-long, we had Kenny Anderson trapped. Elvin Bethea and Curley Culp actually had him sandwiched, but Kenny dipped up between 'em and they (Bethea and Culp) collided. Well, we thought Elvin broke his neck. Thank God, he didn't. Curley was knocked out.

"Well, Kenny was still facin' long yardage and now it was fourth down. Just one more incomplete and we had ourselves a helluva win. But Kenny, on a scramble, hit Isaac Curtis comin' across the middle, and that young man turned in one of the all-time great runs to score. We got beat, 31-27. You always hate to lose, but you *really* hate to lose when you've played hard and deserved to win. Still, Kenny Anderson showed what a great quarterback he was, and is.

"I guess this is as good a time as any to bring this up but I really think we're snakebit in Cincinnati. We've only beaten Cincinnati two out of eight times and *never* in Cincinnati. I don't know why, maybe we try too hard up there. I don't mean that if we tried less, we'd win. What I mean is we try so hard, we tighten up. We have three players from that area — Greg Stemrick, Al Johnson and Rob Carpenter — and Gregg Bingham is from right up the road at Purdue. Then Eddie Biles, our defensive coordinator coached college ball there at Xavier (O.) and is a native of Cincinnati, and our public relations director for four years, Jack Cherry, lived and worked there. All of these people want to beat Cincinnati. Our players want to win for 'em, too. But so much for Cincinnati, and so much for that second year.

Bum began putting the broken pieces back together in 1977, explaining to Dale Robertson of the *Houston Post*, "When you only win five games, you can use help everywhere. We're not lookin' for people to play positions. We're lookin' for good football players."

Bum must have known things were going right. Suddenly Pastorini and Culp stopped talking about leaving town. Houston was no longer purgatory for wayward tackles and ends. The Astrodome was no longer the pits. The Oilers began to feel good about themselves under Bum, who gave them a sense of pride and asked for only a full day's work in return.

"You got a lot of people that will play the *games* under difficult conditions," Bum has come to recognize, "but the thing you gotta have is some people that will *practice* under difficult conditions. I mean when it's hot and they're tired; if they don't get the practice, they're not gonna be as good when they play.

"Ask our scouts. When we go 'round and look at college players, we don't ask if they can play with a little pain. We ask 'em, 'Do they practice with it?' If they practice with it, I know damn well they'll play with it."

It wasn't that long ago that Houston had the reputation for being dog heaven. Some players who didn't want to put out or play hurt became Houston Oilers. Those players would sit around, go through the motions and collect their pensions. The elder statesmen, and this is true on most teams, would have a way of missing Wednesday, Thursday and Friday with a "sore hamstring" only to play all four quarters on Sunday. It's a veteran's definition for the word *veteran*.

"That's where I step in, " Bum assures. "I decide whether it would hurt a guy more to practice. I'm supposed to have enough judgment."

Sometimes it's the weather. The Oilers played a game against Miami in the sultry Orange Bowl on the third Sunday of the '77 season that left Bum something less than proud of his boys. It wasn't so much that they lost 27-7, but they subconsciously tried to save something for the third and fourth quarters because of the heat and humidity that scorched their feet and smarted their eyes.

"Lots of times you don't play real well," Bum understands, "but you should always play hard. In the first quarter of that game, we didn't play well and we didn't play hard, either."

Miami jumped off to a 21-0 lead in the first quarter, and the Oilers were never in the game.

But Bum's boys came back to play both well and hard under adverse conditions in Cleveland on the 13th week of the season, striking a blow for character building. To say the field was unfit for a football game that day would be like saying Manhattan is a poor place to plant a cotton crop. Final score: Houston 19, Cleveland 15.

"It was terrible conditions," Bum recalls. "Nobody but a football player would be fool enough to get out there. that ground was so hard that it was like a pond of ice. The guys couldn't stand up. It takes a special kind of guy to go out on a Sunday afternoon in that kind of weather conditions and play a game like they played. They played hard.

"I don't know how they caught the ball. We intercepted four passes and I don't see how anybody could catch the ball. Their hands were frostbitten. Billy Johnson ran a punt back that nobody in the world could've run back but him, because nobody else could've jumped as high as he did and landed on his feet.

"There's no way you can prepare to play a game like that," Bum has decided, "because there's no way you can practice bein' miserable."

Pastorini and several other Oiler players wore ski masks under their helmets. "And a whole bunch more would've liked to have had 'em but they weren't available. We knew it was gonna be cold. But not havin' been exposed to a whole lot of that kind of weather, we didn't have no idea just how cold it was. I mean it was bad. You had to have some kind of protection in your face. The quarterback, doin' as much talkin' and audiblin' and signal callin' and everything, he's gotta keep his ol' jaws where he can move 'em. Everybody else could just grunt. Dan had to speak.

"It was cold enough to freeze your muscles. I'll tell ya, I never seen a football field like that. The ground was so thick with ice that they had bulldozers out there before the game, and they didn't even make a dent. If you fall the right way, you break your arm. Boom! Just like that, 'cause it was uneven, not smooth like an ice rink. It had little uneven waves that were frozen.

"Gol-lee, and the players never even thought about it. They didn't sit around and dread it and all that. What the hell, it's a game and they're obligated to play. They *wanted* to play. They didn't want it to be cold but our football team likes to play football."

A lot of unpleasant things happened to the Oilers in 1977. It was a season of pain and Blue Cross. Dan Pastorini was forced to leave the Oilers' 27-10 victory over Pittsburgh because of a severely sprained ankle that made walking afterwards as much a challenge as finding a way beforehand to beat the Steelers. Then Elvin Bethea broke his arm after having played in a team-record 135 straight games for the Oilers.

Bum and his assistants had to coach harder than they ever coached before.

"I don't mean to brag," Bum says, "but I feel we did a better job of coachin' than we done my first couple of years. We had some good football players, understand, but a lot of 'em were so damn young that we had to make some adjustments. You couldn't ask 'em to do too many things.

"There's a tendency in football to think of more things than you can do. In the beginnin' of the year, we probably had them doin' too much. Eventually, we got back to basics. They learned as a unit, and we progressed as a unit."

By the fourteenth and final week of the season, the Oilers were primed to prove something, if nothing more than they could beat a football team that couldn't afford to lose, the Cincinnati Bengals.

To set the scene, Cincinnati (8-5) came into the Astrodome in need of a victory to advance to the AFC playoffs; a loss or a tie spelled Pittsburgh instead. It was that cut-and-dried. It was that important to the Bengals. But Bum convinced the Oilers (7-6) that they, too, had to win in order to have a winning season. Furthermore, even though they couldn't gain the playoffs, the Oilers could wrestle second place away from Cincinnati under the complicated NFL tie-breaker system.

"We had played only two real bad ball games in my first three years as head coach here, and those two were on Monday Night Football. We wanted to do good so bad, but we didn't have the poise or confidence. So now the whole United States was waitin' to see what we were gonna do against Cincinnati," Bum recalls.

"Here we had a chance to change the whole race. We couldn't win it but we had a chance to beat the team that *was* gonna win it, and that's the same thing as winnin' it in a way. Up to that point in time, this ball game meant more to our team than any football game we had played. To me, it meant more than any football game I'd ever been in. Everybody was watchin' to see if we were gonna fall flat on our face again."

The Houston Oilers became the Houston Spoilers that afternoon by beating the Bengals 21-16, as Billy Johnson held his own "How To" football clinic, catching six passes for 138 yards, rushing once for 31 yards and returning kicks for another 94 yards. And when it was all over, Billy had more all-purpose yardage (263) than the Bengals had total offense (228).

"Billy Johnson had one of the greatest days ever by a player in a single game, and our defense literally ran Kenny Anderson right to the bench in the fourth quarter," Bum recalls affectionately. "It might be the only day, other than maybe one other time, that we have contained a quarterback of his stature so well and just really shut him down like that.

"Kenny Anderson and John Shinners, one of their guards, had some nice things to say about our team after that game. I know both of 'em sincerely meant it, because they are both the kind of people that are a credit to the game and mean what they say. I recall Kenny sayin', 'Gee, now I know what people mean when they say a tough day at the office.' I don't mean to harp on this one game but, in reality, it was the biggest win we'd ever had as a team and as a staff up to that point. And it carried over to the next season.

"I don't gloat over the fact that we knocked Cincinnati out of the divisional championship and a playoff spot, and neither do our players. Instead, that was the day we learned how to win, how to win the big game, how to win the game that everyone was watchin' across the country. A lot was made about it bein' a 'get-even game' for our loss on a blown call earlier in the year at Cincinnati. That was not true. We wanted to win that game for ourselves and for the people of Houston. Hell, one of my best friends was their coach, Bill (Tiger) Johnson. I would've loved to seen Tiger in the playoffs. But friendship was out the window and, if the situation had been reversed, Tiger would've done the same thing to me.

"People will remember that the Commissioner had 'apologized' to me for the call in the Cincinnati game and, for eight or six weeks, we never mentioned the conversation. But then Mr. Rozelle disclosed it himself at a game he was attendin' a few weeks before and so it was out of the bag. But the second game with Cincinnati was already a fired-up game for us. I think what really hurt 'em was one of their players sayin' a few days before the game, 'Houston will play tough for awhile, then they'll fold their tents like always.' That was a big mistake. Our players knew that he was sayin' we'd choke or that we couldn't play the good teams. Nothin' will fire up a team more than to have an opposin' player say somethin' like that."

Actually, Coy Bacon was the Bengal whose mouth inspired the Oilers. Cincinnati had just beaten Pittsburgh the week before and, in the roar of the winning locker room, Bacon was asked if the Bengals could now beat the Oilers. "We just beat the best," came the smug reply. "How is Houston gonna stop us?"

"As far as we're concerned, that was a great year for us," Bum says of '77. "We really started to put things together. We had a great draft. We had traded Lynn Dickey to Green Bay for a draft pick and also got Kenny Ellis, who we turned around and dealt away to Miami for an early draft pick. We went into the '77 draft with a No. 1, a No. 2 and three No. 3s. We took Mo Towns on the first, George Reihner on the second, and got Rob Carpenter and Timmy Wilson in the third. What a great group. Timmy and Rob gave us a pair of runnin' backs to go with Ronnie Coleman and Don Hardeman; Mo and George became our future on the offensive line.

"We were too young to get a wild card and we weren't ready to win a divisional championship, but, hell, we didn't play like we knew that. We went a long way, damn near all the way to the playoffs. But we were really young. I think when we started that season, we had more rookies and second year players than anybody in the league, except for Tampa Bay and Seattle. We were so green that I think the cows were ready to eat us. We struggled, every week we struggled. But, as they say, the chemistry was there. The kids blended with the veterans so well, and vice versa, and they eventually ignited us into becomin' a fireball team.

"Anyway, we kinda bounced our way along that year; Cincinnati was doin' the same, and so was Pittsburgh. We beat Pittsburgh early in the Dome and that was another big win for the franchise. We were tellin' the world that we've got ourselves a team. Just how good, we didn't know. But look out, because we were gonna play people tough. I think by '78, other teams knew."

He's A Jekyll And Hyde

Obviously, the Atlanta Falcons weren't impressed. They handed the Oilers a 20-14 loss in the first game of the '78 season when most people across the country still didn't know whether it was Leeman Bennett or Bennett Leeman.

"As it turned out," Bum recollects, "Atlanta was a good enough football team that it wasn't a disgrace to get beat by 'em. But at the time, nobody knew it. That's why beatin' Kansas City the followin' week (20-17) was so important because we shouldn't have been oh-and-two against Atlanta and Kansas City. That would've been tough mentally as well as bein' oh-and-two in the standings. You gotta beat the teams you're better than and hope you can break even with the teams that are better'n you . . . and I thought we were better than both of them.

"I tell my players, 'Don't expect somebody else to win for you.' We started buildin' that up four years ago or whenever we got a new player. 'It's your obligation,' I tell 'em. 'Whatever the team needs, that's what you gotta prepare yourself to do. Individually, you gotta do any damn thing you can to help this football team, includin' leadership, includin' self-discipline.' Now you don't start that in the middle of a year. The majority of our good players didn't just happen last year."

After splitting with Atlanta and Kansas City, the Oilers beat San Francisco by one point, lost to Los Angeles by four, beat Cleveland by three, lost to Oakland by four, and beat Buffalo and Pittsburgh each by seven before losing to Cincinnati 28-13. They had come off an exhausting Monday Night TV victory over the Steelers and ran into a Bengal team that was 0-8 and grossly overdue. The Oilers regrouped, beating Cleveland by four, New England by three (after trailing 23-0 in the second quarter) and Miami by five. They were on their way to the AFC playoffs.

"We got into the playoffs as a wildcard team," Bum recalls, "and right off we had to play Miami in Miami. I figure we gotta run the ball 45-50 times. If we do that, I think we can win. But we're crippled like hell. They got a quarterback (Bob Griese) crippled but we're crippled all over."

Final score: Houston 17, Miami 9.

The Dolphins concentrated on stopping the Oilers' running game and left the passing lanes unattended. Dan Pastorini, wearing a flak jacket to protect damaged ribs, completed 20 of 29 passes for 306 yards. Earl Campbell finished with 84 yards on 26 rushes, a modest (for him) 3.2 average.

"Our guys didn't luck out," Bum reminds. "We took the ball game away. We had won a pressure game against Cincinnati the second time around, against Miami durin' the season, against Pittsburgh durin' the season. But that playoff game against Miami was more important to this franchise than any of 'em because it was bigger than any of 'em. By comparison, everythin' else was like a preseason game.

"You should've seen the reception we got when we got back to Houston that night. The airport people didn't want our players walkin' through the airport because fans were double-parked and triple-parked, waitin' for us. So we decided to get off the plane, get on a bus and come straight to the Oiler office down the street from our practice field. Well, the fans found out and they were in the street waitin' for us. In fact, we had to stop a block from the buildin' because there was 5,000, 6,000, maybe 7,000 people. I'm talkin' about a *sea* of people, a hundred yards deep. You couldn't move; you couldn't sign autographs, and when Earl got off the bus, it's lucky he had any clothes left. Everybody wanted a piece of shirt, a necklace, anythin' they could get their hands on."

New England was next. Carl Mauck, a very funny fellow who plays center for the Oilers and resembles Billy Carter without glasses (which may or may not be relevant to his behavior), decided to compose a fight song. He not only set his piece of pseudo-poetry to music (to the tune of *Wabash Cannonball*) but sang it himself.

Mauck, a 32-year-old, off-the-wall opportunist, hired a small band, found himself a recording studio and crooned his little jingle about the Houston Oilers personified. Most folks agreed: It wasn't pretty but it sang. *Oiler Cannonball* cracked the Top 40 charts of at least one Houston radio station after only two days.

"From sunny Miami, Florida, To icy
Boston, Mass.,
From the Broncos of Colorado, To
the iron in the Steelers' masks.
He's mighty tough and rugged, He's
feared quite well by all.
He's the winning combination of
the Oiler Cannonball.
Here's to Head Coach Phillips,
May his name forever stand,
And always be remembered, By the
fans throughout the land.
When the Super Bowl is over,
And those Cowboys finally fall,
We'll carry him home to Houston,
On the Oiler Cannonball.
Listen to the blockin', The ramblin'
and the roar,
As he glides along the sidelines,
By the hashmarks for the score.
From the fancy passin' dago, To the
Tyler (Texas) bowling ball,
Those Patriots can be taken,
By the Oiler Cannonball."

This is the same Carl Mauck who informed Earl Campbell when a Cincinnati sportswriter approached the reticent rookie earlier in the season, "Be careful, all sportswriters are Communists." This is the same Carl Mauck who plays every football game as if it meant the Super Bowl. This is the same Carl Mauck from McLeansboro, Ill.

Oiler Cannonball became a smash and, at the same time, exposed Mauck as a singer. He was a better prophet. Both Bum and Dan Pastorini encouraged him never to forget how to snap a football. That's what friends are for. Pastorini and Mauck are as close as peanut butter and jelly, as Bum puts it, but that doesn't mean Dan has to buy his records.

"Mauck might be another Tiny Tim," Bum mused. "I know one thing, he's bad. That's why he can't miss."

"Yeah," Pastorini nodded, "he sings better when he's drinking."

"Hmmmmmph," Bum sniffed. "Mauck's the kind of singer you gotta drink along with, so you *won't* mind him."

Carl Mauck: 6-4, 250 . . . fifth-year Oiler, 11th-year pro . . . graduated from Southern Illinois with honors, 4.57 out of a possible 5.0 in business management . . . selected by Baltimore 13 round, 1969 . . . traded by San Diego Chargers to Houston Oilers for the negotiating rights to guard Booker Brown and defensive back Benny Johnson.

This was Bum's first trade as head coach and general manager of the Oilers. It was a steal. Mauck would become to the offensive line what Curley Culp became to the defensive line: a durable player, a willing teacher, a responsible leader, a basic fulcrum upon which a line can be built left and right.

I've never seen a guy as intense in a football game as Carl Mauck," Bum praises. "Before the game and after the game he's an angel; durin' the game he's a devil. I mean he's a Jekyll and Hyde. He gets in a game, he don't know who it is, don't *care* who it is. If you're on his football field, you aggravate him.

"He's the best natural leader — other than John Hadl — that I've been around. Just natural. He don't try to be a leader. He's not a rah-rah guy; he leads by doin' things. A couple of years ago, George Reihner came right out of college and started for us at guard. That's unheard of for an offensive lineman, but one of the reasons he did it was Carl Mauck. I mean Carl Mauck worked with him during the off-season and right on through the season. He's got our offensive line goin' like you can't believe."

Indeed, this still relatively unheralded offensive line has grown to provide the best pass protection in the National Football League, allowing an NFL low of 17 sacks in 1978. Left tackle Greg Sampson, an eight-year veteran from Stanford, has been lost for the '79 season with brain surgery; however, the Oilers went out and acquired All-Pro tackle Leon Gray from the New England Patriots in exchange for a pair of 1980 draft choices, a first and a sixth.

Bum wants to win. He has combed the waiver wires and made four significant trades to mold this team into a serious contender. Rich Caster came from the New York Jets for draft choices. Draft rights for Earl Campbell were obtained from the Tampa Bay Bucs for Jimmy Giles and draft choices. Mauck was a gimme. Now Gray from the Pats for more draft choices.

There are only 13 players left from the 1974 team which Bum inherited: Ken Burrough, Greg Sampson, Billy Johnson, Ed Fisher, Dan Pastorini, Ronnie Coleman, Elvin Bethea, Curley Culp, Gregg Bingham, Willie Alexander, C.L. Whittington, Steve Kiner and Ted Washington.

"Time is very limited in trainin' camp," Bum notes, "and that's the only reason I don't coach on the field. I stand back where I can see everybody, everyday, every minute of every practice. Somebody's got to make the decision of who's the most important players to our football team. I look for little things. The way a guy takes correction is important to me.

"We're not always right. We drafted Steve Largent in '76 and I've been lookin' for an excuse why we traded him ever since. We blew it. We didn't judge him right. Maybe we had our minds made up before we went on the field, I don't know. We had pretty good receivers that year but that's no excuse. Tradin' away Steve Largent was a big mistake, and I swore then I was never gonna cut a player before he proved to me that he could not play. When you screw up, you screw up. You just hope like the devil you don't make many mistakes like that.

"A lot of other people around the league have made mistakes with some of the guys we have on our football team, or else we wouldn't have 19 free agents. We traded Largent for an eight round draft choice and we got Eddie Foster in the eighth round. Eddie Foster played every game for us his rookie year . . . but I would've liked to have had both of 'em, Largent and Foster.

"Scouting is so damn important. How much are you gonna write about this? But my son, Wade, is a heckuva judge of talent. I don't want to embarrass him. But he knows football players, and he stands by what he says. I like that. Don't make a mistake of not bein' decisive. If it's wrong, make the damn decision, or you'll end up bein' right in the middle on everythin'. If a guy's right in the middle, he don't have no beliefs at all.

"Scouting and organization. You can damn-near take any-body and let him coach if he can organize. And leave him there and let him get his theory goin' and let him have an off year or two. If you have just average intelligence, you got a good chance of buildin' a good team. That's the thing that hurts most people. They won't let anybody stay in power long enough to build somethin'. They got it about halfway done, then let somebody else come in. Invariably, they don't like it the way it was and so they change it. It keeps everythin' in a constant turmoil."

Bum is under the impression that building a football team is more like working a crossword puzzle than collecting stamps.

"If you took the very best 22 guys in the league, I don't think you could win," Bum maintains. "I mean the best offensive left guard, the best center, the best right guard, etc. Because you'd have 22 individuals. I think you can take a good football team like us or Pittsburgh or Dallas and beat that 22 individuals. I just believe you can have too many stars on a football team, like you can have too few.

"That's my opinion," he shrugs. "There's no way to prove it, so I guess my opinion counts."

Bum is a fanatic for detail. He has Earl Campbell, but he also has Johnnie Dirden and Guido Merkens. He can field a $1 million offense and, at the same time, appreciate the dedication and expertise of an Al Johnson on the special teams. "Al Johnson can't run as fast as a lot of people on our kickoff team," Bum says, "but he beats 'em all downfield."

Special team players. They are so "special" that the average fan can't name five of them on the punt coverage unit of his favorite football team. Special teamers (except for the return men) are as anonymous as head linesmen. However, Bum places the same kind of importance on special team players as the Dallas Cowboy cheerleading committee places on beautiful women.

Basically, Bum looks for young men who consider their cra-niums to be part of the standard equipment used to bring a ball carrier to his knees in the open field, quickly and cleanly, the way Tom Ferguson wrestles ornery rodeo steers to the ground. Bum rates heart above press clippings. He prefers pumped-up and possessed to pretty and polite.

"To make a good special teamer, a guy has got to want to be on the special teams," Bum explains. "He's got to feel that's part of the game, and it is. Twenty-five per cent of the game is special teams. You gotta find guys who will accept that challenge.

"This whole league is made up of people who just assume they're gonna go out and do the job, whatever that may be. They never even hesitate. They just do it. Everybody talks about drugs — which started way back — but they're not givin' the athletes enough credit.

"Billy Currier is that way. He can't hardly tell you his name on the football field, and God knows he's never taken nothin'. He was that way in college. Kurt Knoff is the same way. Some people get psyched up and, oh boy, I mean they're psyched up. They go out there and they ain't takin' nothing. Carl Mauck will compete in a handball game like it meant life or death. I mean life or death. He's learned to get hisself up for a game . . . and he does it."

Special teams are basically suicide squads, missions of mercy, knee donors. Perhaps it's his humble upbringing, which taught unselfishness and sacrifice, but Bum can relate to these unsung warriors.

Then there's Billy (White Shoes) Johnson.

"He's one helluva special team all by hisself," Bum says.

"When Billy gets his hands on the ball, the main thing is to get out of his way because there's no tellin' when he's gonna come back in your direction. When Billy gets his hands on the ball, it's 'look-out' time. We don't even know where he's gonna go.

"That guy is fantastic. He's a great athlete. He can really catch the football; if he can touch it, he can catch it. It don't make any difference whether they're under him, over him, and if you don't hit him the instant he catches the ball . . . well, it's adios. He'll run off with it and hide.

"As far as that little dance he does in the end zone, he's a favorite of so many people that he can do damn near what he wants to. They might not like it if somebody else did it. But he can do it. He can do anything. I don't know what the word is. He's

such a *natural* that everybody loves him. They're all waitin' after
the game for his autograph. I get on the bus pretty quick. The
only question they ask me is 'when's Billy comin' out?'

"He can do things with a football nobody else can do. He's
made some of the most fantastic runs I've ever seen, and I'm not
prejudiced that way. I respect a good player whether it's a
Bradshaw or a Green or a Sipe. I don't care who it is. But this kid
has made better moves with a football on punt returns and things.
He don't have a *few* of 'em; he's got a *bunch* of 'em."

There was one move Billy Johnson tried to make that Bum
forbade. White Shoes planned to sit home during a contract dispute with Oiler management during training camp '78.

"I've always hated to get involved in contract negotiations,"
Bum explains. "If you're right for the player, obviously you're
wrong for the owner. If you're right for the owner, you're wrong
for the player. So I just try to stay out of 'em."

However, this was one contract squabble that Bum did get
himself involved.

"Billy Johnson can't hardly do anythin' that I wouldn't
approve of. What I mean is that it would be hard for Billy to make
me mad. But I didn't approve of him not bein' in camp just 'cause
he had a contract dispute. I told him that. If he does it, and I let
him get away with doin' it, then 12 more guys won't show up
next year. It was goin' to set a precedent that I couldn't afford to
have set."

So Billy White Shoes made one of his patented returns to the
Oiler Cannonball. Bum carries clout. Unfortunately, a knee in-
jury would put Billy's dance on the shelf for '78, which makes the
Oilers' accomplishments that season even more remarkable.

New England fell, 31-14, in Chuck Fairbank's last game as
head coach of the Patriots. It wasn't close. "We've never been
here before," Pastorini blinked afterwards. "It's kinda like a fairy
tale." For the Oiler Cannonball, it was onto the AFC championship game against Pittsburgh.

"We expect a knock-down, drag-out fight," Bum drawled.
"We're gonna sever diplomatic relations with 'em. That's what
you do when you're declarin' war, isn't it?"

Countdown To Catastrophe

For Earl Campbell, the trauma that the Houston Oilers would experience in Pittsburgh on January 7, 1979, began with a press conference the morning before the AFC Championship Game. "Earl hates to be interviewed in front of a crowd," Bum would explain later. "He'd rather take a beatin' first."

On Friday night, the Oilers checked into a Marriott, located about 20 minutes from downtown Pittsburgh on the way from the airport. AFC Director of Public Relations Joe Browne had scheduled a press conference for 9 a.m. Saturday at the downtown William Penn Hotel, which was media headquarters. He had asked Bum to bring along a couple of his boys. Namely Dan Pastorini and Earl Campbell.

Bum knew how much his quarterback would enjoy a good herd of journalists and how reticent his rookie running back would be. Nevertheless, he asked both of them to be in the lobby at 8:30 the next morning.

"Obviously, Earl was nervous because he stayed up lookin' at the late shows," Bum discovered. "When Bob Hyde, our assistant PR director, woke him the next morning, Earl told him, 'I'm so tired. I'm worn out. I can't go.' Bob asked me if he should call him back and I said, 'Don't worry about it.' Sure enough, five minutes before we were ready to leave, Earl was in the lobby ready to go."

A bus was waiting outside to take them to the William Penn. Dan and Bum kibitzed across the aisle. Earl never uttered a word. "Tight as a drum," Bum observed privately. "It ain't the football games that make him that way; it's havin' to answer a question to someone he don't know."

On the other hand, Pastorini not only appeared anxious to meet the press but he succeeded in looking better than anyone else in the room that morning. That was a small feat, perhaps, since his fur coat and baby blue cowboy hat with oversized peacock feathers were simply no match for a room filled with balding heads, cardigan sweaters and polyester knit pants.

Bum spoke first.

"I expect a hard-fought game, I expect a clean game. We've never played the Pittsburgh Steelers in anythin' but a clean game. Other than that, I can't make a helluva lot of predictions at 9 o'clock in the morning."

The respect and admiration that Bum has for the Steelers had to have a seed, a beginning, a first impression. The year was 1974 and the impression was made by Mean Joe Greene.

"I'll never forget," Bum will tell you. "We played Pittsburgh and we beat 'em up there. They needed that ball game. They hadn't won the Super Bowl yet and they were strugglin' to get into the playoffs. We beat 'em in a ball game that had to mean a whole lot to them, a lot more to them than it did to us because we were out of it.

"Well, Joe Greene came up to me after the game and said, 'Coach, be sure to congratulate ol' No. 7 (Pastorini) because he's been through a whole lot and he's never gotten down. He's always gotten up off the ground and he hasn't had a lot of (pass) protection. He's a real competitor. I'm proud for him.' Here he was genuinely hurtin' because they just got beat but, at the same time, he could be proud for somebody else. The Terry Bradshaws, the Joe Greenes, a lot of 'em in this league . . . hell, they're the same kind of people we got. They're the same players we got 'cept they got a different color hat on."

Pastorini spoke next.

"Earl Campbell? Well, Bum said a long time ago that Earl Campbell gave the Houston Oilers a sword to fight with. He gave us a dimension we never had before."

Reporters scribbled notes between enormous intakes of hot coffee. "Dan, what are you doing differently this year that makes you better?" one of them asked.

Pastorini nodded matter-of-factly toward Campbell. "Givin' the ball to him."

Everyone laughed. Even Campbell smiled, although he would still rather take a beating. When he did speak, his comments were brief: either "yes" or "no" or "Bum can answer that."

Pastorini continued: "When they start giving me the punishment, I give Earl the ball and let him take the punishment for awhile. I think this will be the most physical game we'll ever play. To me, I feel this is the Super Bowl. I think the best two teams in the National Football League will be playing tomorrow."

There had been earlier comments made by the Cincinnati Bengals after suffering a late-season loss to the Oilers that made the stubble stand up on the back of Bum's neck. Gary Burley, a defensive end, was asked about Campbell's 27 rushes for 122 yards that day. "He's got so much determination," Burley began. "But I hope he doesn't run like this his whole career because I don't think he can last that long. Maybe I'm wrong. Maybe he's Superman. But I haven't seen many who have run like that for 10 years."

This was brought up at the Saturday morning press conference and Bum swallowed what he really wanted to say. Instead, he simply assured the questioner that "a guy's body is not gonna wear out just because he runs hard" and that football is a game where "you have to be the hitter, not the hittee." Burley's quotes bugged him, but Bum wouldn't make an issue of it.

Then somebody asked him to explain the Oilers' success in games away from the Astrodome. Bum thought about that a moment, chewed a little, then replied, "I tell 'em I'm gonna leave 'em if they don't win."

"What do you think about Bum Phillips?" Pastorini was asked.

The Hollywood-handsome quarterback of the Cinderella Oilers absorbed the question, then slowly turned to Bum. "Will you," he directed, "leave the room?"

The Oilers are an emotional bunch who play football for a man who admits to crying over *Brian's Song* and confesses that he is a sucker for sad movies and little kids. In turn, the players also wear their feelings right on their shoulder pads for the world to see. They are honest and open. It was time for a straight-forward testimonial about the coach.

"He's like my second father," Pastorini said. "We have a lot of respect, a lot of love for each other. We holler at each other, but it doesn't last long. Bum is the finest man I've ever had the pleasure to work with."

Bum fidgeted uncomfortably in his seat. When he couldn't think of anything funny or fitting to say, he fielded the next question about the Oilers' practice routine.

"Football has got to be fun," Bum told his audience. "We don't scrimmage each other. We don't go 11-on-11. But when I say that, people assume we don't practice hard. That's not really true but I realize it makes a better story.

"I never said what *we* do is the only way of doin' things. Some teams run wind sprints; I don't. That's why they make chocolate and vanilla."

At this point, Bum felt the press conference was over. "I about run out of soap, men," he said, standing up and grabbing his cowboy hat. Suddenly there was a crowd around him. This wasn't a press conference; this was sheer entertainment. The newspapermen couldn't get enough. They wouldn't let him leave, perhaps already fearing the prospects of covering a Super Bowl coached by Chuck Noll on one side and Tom Landry on the other.

"What would you think of an all-Texas Super Bowl?" Bum was asked.

"The world's not ready for it," he replied. "You think we're obnoxious now, you just wait and see."

Bum stood for another 15 minutes, discussing such topics as the origin of his nickname, the calloused branches of his family tree, the joys of his 28-stall horse barn in Missouri City, and the long and winding road from coaching football at Nederland High School to being one game away from Super Bowl XIII.

"I started so damn low in this business," he drawled. "I mean if you started where I did, coachin' the B-squad, you'd know what I mean. They're not exactly knockin' on your door."

"Did you have dreams of someday coaching in the NFL?"

"Hell I never knew they had pro ball."

"How hard is it to get that first job?"

"Well, it's a closed group. They don't think you can coach in the league unless you've played pro ball. That's not true. There's teaching teachin' and coachin' involved in coachin'."

"What kind of a player were you?"

"I thought I was real good until I looked back and saw a film of me. Most disappointin' experience I ever had."

"What position?"

"I was a fullback but they played me at guard. Poor

coachin'."

"Any scholarship offers from college?"

"Not much demand for 185-pound linemen."

"So what did you do after high school?"

"I joined the Marine Corps. I learned my lesson. I never joined anything else the rest of my life. I went in as a private and, 31 months later, I came out as a private. I thought they couldn't win that war without me. Then I got in there and I thought they couldn't win *because* of me. The Marine Corps was real spit'n polish. I wasn't."

The bus was parked outside. Politely, Bum finally excused himself and made his way through the lobby to the exit. He seemed slightly out of place with his sheepskin coat and red kangaroo boots, parading through the charming old Victorian lobby with crystal chandeliers and ornate wood carvings. Dennis Weaver never played it better. Reporters' pens bobbed in his wake. It was time to say goodbye. Bum just nodded and said "so long."

That afternoon, the Oilers held a 30-minute workout at Three Rivers. It was a chance for the players to adapt to the subfreezing temperatures. It was also a chance for Bum to give Terry Bradshaw a black cowboy hat with a thin gold string band that he had brought from Houston. Size 7 5/8. A gift. His motive? He likes Terry Bradshaw.

"Still, I'm gonna have Dan give it to him'" Bum decided, "so it doesn't look like I'm bribin' him."

So Pastorini delivered the hat prior to the Oilers' workout. He wrote across the top of the box: Happy New Year. Let's Go Huntin'. This Is From Bum And Me." He set it in Bradshaw's locker and left.

It was a very robust 20 degrees outdoors that afternoon. Earl Campbell sipped a cup of coffee while he slowly dressed in one corner of the visitors' locker room. Bum stayed bundled in his sheepskin coat as he talked to reporters.

"Playin' Pittsburgh is like eatin' an ice cream cone on a hot, summer day," Bum analogized. "Sometime before you can get it all in your mouth, it gets all over ya."

Somebody asked him about Donnie Shell's hit on Campbell

in the December 3 Steeler-Oiler game, a collision that resulted in a fractured rib for the Houston running back.

"Earl had his eighth rib broken," Bum explained. "When he fell, he broke it. Lookin' at the film, Shell hit him as he turned in the air and, when Earl came down, he came down flat on his back like a pancake. That's what broke his rib. It wasn't the lick."

There was a momentary pause. "Not takin' anything away from Donnie Shell," Bum added, "because he's sure as hell capable of breakin' a rib.

"I've got to go now, if there aren't anymore questions. I've got a football team on the field. I'm not really important to them . . . but they think I am."

Mike Barber, the brawny tight end who had caught nine passes for a 21.7-yard average and two touchdowns in the first two playoff victories, decided to work out in a T-shirt.

"Hey, Woody Hayes," Bum called to him.

"It's all mental," Barber shrugged. "This is what I'll be wearin' tomorrow, so I better get used to it."

"I like what Mike Barber tells reporters who wanna know how we got this far," Bum smiled. "Mike tells 'em, 'We've been climbing a tall mountain with a short rope all season.' "

Gregg Bingham, most macho Oiler of them all, wasn't to be outdone. He wore a pair of shorts that afternoon. It was a spirited workout. Bum hooted and hollered right along with his players. Rodeo sounds they made. The field was dry, the Oilers were loose and the head coach was at the top of his game. But when the workout was over, even Barber and Bingham were ready to take a hot shower.

"We wanna get gone," Bum told reporters who began milling around his players afterward. "We wanna get out of here before we freeze . . . (pausing) get out of this weather that I keep sayin' won't make any difference tomorrow."

Even the Steeler players seemed to be staring at Bum, ironic because that's the way people used to stare at Jack Lambert and Dwight White when they first captured the heart and attention of national television audiences four years earlier. Enigmas, all of them. They seemed to appreciate this common cowboy with the colorful quips, perhaps because they saw in Bum Phillips the antithesis of their own head coach.

"I like his boots," said White, a Texan himself who might be slightly prejudiced. "He's very loose and the players say they have a lot of fun. I'm glad to see it. It puts a new wrinkle in that normal NFL coaching style. At first, you want to take him as a joke. But Bum ain't no bum."

White and Bum had something in common during the week of the AFC Championship Game. Both of them had some fun while conjuring up thoughts of a Houston-Dallas Super Bowl.

"If that happens," White warned, "the State of Texas will file for sovereignty. They'll secede from the Union. Knowin' all the money and influence they've got down there, they'll have the game moved. They'll tell the league, 'The hell with Miami, we're playin' it in Austin!' "

On the eve of the biggest game of Bum's coaching career, he sat in his room and had a few beers. "We've come on somethin' here that we've never been through before," he said with some concern in his voice. "There is more interest, more writers, more television people than we're used to seein'. I cautioned the players about that. If they're gonna stop and sign autographs 25 minutes at a time, that's fine, unless it puts their minds on somethin' else. That's the only thing I'm worried about."

He reminded them, "We got here by bein' a lot of little people, not by bein' big people. In this game, the minute you lose, everythin' goes out the window. So don't let it go to your head."

When Bum turned in that night, he thought his team was ready for the Steelers.

The Behinder We Got, The Worse It Got

Three Rivers Stadium took on all the charm of cold concrete and soggy synthetic turf by the time the American Football Conference championship was on the line Sunday. The temperature was 26 degrees and a steady, icy rain made playing conditions something less than ideal. Shelly Winters had better footing in the *Poseidon Adventure*.

Nevertheless, Bum was in fine spirits as he walked onto the spongy, water-soaked field to observe pre-game warmups from the end zone. He wore a clear plastic covering on his cowboy hat to protect it from the elements. Looking around the stadium, he noticed one sign out of more than a hundred signs hanging from the facade:

"Don't Send A Bum To Miami."

Bum pointed it out to several of his associates and laughed. "I like that," he kept saying. "I like that." But he didn't like what would happen to his Oilers that afternoon. They won the coin toss, and that was the last thing to go their way.

At the end of the first quarter, Franco Harris had scored on a seven-yard sweep and Rocky Bleier on a 17-yard sweep. Earl Campbell had rushed nine times for 13 yards, including four losses and two fumbles. The Steelers had netted 118 yards to the Oilers' 12. The Steelers had scored 14 points to the Oilers' zero.

Then, on the very first play of the second quarter, Mike Barber was cut at the knees by Steeler safety Mike Wagner on an overthrown pass from Pastorini. Barber lay in obvious pain on the cold, clammy turf. His right knee throbbed. He was done for the day. Barber, who had to be assisted from the field, didn't leave without pointing a menacing finger and shouting a few get-even obscenities in Wagner's direction. It was an ugly scene.

But this was a game of ugly scenes. There was Elvin Bethea's two-point takedown of Jon Kolb, Richard Caster's shoving match with Mel Blount, Ken Burrough's scuffle with Ron Johnson and, the ugliest of all, Barber's violent collision with Wagner.

"I had total respect for Mike Wagner comin' into this game," Barber bit off the words afterwards. "I don't have none anymore."

Toni Fritsch kicked a 19-yard field goal to cut the Steeler lead to 14-3, and that's the way it stayed until inside the two-minute warning of the first half. Then came a replay of the Alamo, staged in the final 1:23 of the first half, featuring three Oiler fumbles (including one by Johnny Dirden on a kickoff with nobody within 10 yards of him) and 17 Steeler points. In 48 seconds, the score ballooned from 14-3 to 31-3.

As Bum put it, "The behinder we got, the worse it got." The game plan was obsolete. Pastorini was sacked four times and intercepted five times. Campbell finished with a 2.8-yard average on 22 carries. "At one point," Bethea recalled in a tearful scenario, "I told myself, 'I'm gonna retire after this game.' "

Final score: Pittsburgh 34, Houston 5.

Then, as if watching his team slip-slidin' away wasn't punishment enough, Bum had his $50 cowboy hat pilfered by one of several hundred overzealous fans who were permitted to storm onto the field after the game. Oh, Bum got his hat back, but only after he and one of his players bulldogged the fleeing fan from behind.

"There was absolutely no police protection on the field. It was terrible," Bum groused. "There's a league rule that you're supposed to supply police protection at all your games. They should know better here. They've won enough. If it had happened at our place, maybe I could understand. We didn't know what the fans would do. But this isn't the first time they've won here."

Furthermore, Bum didn't appreciate the fact that he and his players were pelted by snowballs during the game. "It's not that you can get hurt. Snowballs can't hurt ya. It's just that you ought'n be subjected to that." He sighed. "I always say, 'Class will tell.' I guess it did today . . . I'm talkin' about the fans (not the players)."

It was a gruesome afternoon. Angelo Dundee would've thrown in the towel but the Houston Oilers kept playing. Barber's knee wasn't damaged as badly as they had suspected; Bethea wasn't retiring; Bum's hat was safely in hand, and it never rains inside the Astrodome. Things were already looking up as Bum began looking back:

"I hated to play under those conditions but, in all fairness to the Pittsburgh Steelers, it rained on both sides of the football. It was just as cold on their bench as it was on ours. I'll tell ya, that day it would've been hard on a dry field to beat 'em. They were hot. They were *really* hot. Terry was throwin' the ball in the cold, freezin' rain and John Stallworth and Lynn Swann were catchin' it like it was dry. It didn't affect them; it affected us. Both physically and mentally, it affected us.

"But that's part of bein' a champion. You have to overcome the elements and do good anyhow. I have a lot of respect for them for bein' able to do that. I don't like to lose, but I ain't gonna blame somebody else for it . . . not the Good Lord, I'm not gonna blame Him. If He wants it to rain, let it rain.

"I just like to see how it would've come out if we came back at the half, 14-3 or 16-6, instead of 31-3. We got the football and we're goin' down the field with it. We got a chance to get either a field goal or a touchdown before the half. We're down on their 35 or 40 yard line. All of a sudden, we not only don't have the football but we're down 31-3 in 48 seconds. Everything happened all at once. The worst things you can imagine.

"Ice and wet fields hurt Earl because he don't run straight up. Franco does, but Earl don't. When Earl turns a corner, his feet are out here and his shoulders are over there. He's leanin' all the time. You knew damn well his feet were gonna go out from under him, which they did. It not only affects a man's runnin' but he's always afraid he's *gonna* slip.

"Halftime? We were down 31-3, friend. There ain't no way you can go into a locker room and tell grown men, 'Now look, here are the World Champion Pittsburgh Steelers. We're 31-3 behind but we're gonna catch up.' You can't go in and make that kind of pep talk. They ain't gonna believe ya. I just told 'em, 'Let's don't kid ourselves, to win it would take a miracle. We're out of it. Now it's just a matter of how much pride we got.'

"I guess I'm takin' all the romance out of it for everybody. People think halftime is pep talks and all that strategy. You can't go in at halftime and put in new plays or change a bunch of things. Just get all the plays that ain't workin' out of your mind and concentrate on the ones that are workin', and you can do that on the blackboard.

"Well, we were a good second-half football team the whole damn year, but I was as proud of our people the second half of that Pittsburgh game as any game all season. We played hard the second half. I'll guarantee ya, our guys were layin' it on the line the last two minutes of the game. That made me proud that a guy can force hisself to go and do somethin' when there's no reward for it. It's easy to play hard the second half when that ball game will get ya in the playoffs or get ya some extra money. This game was over, except we had to finish it.

"That damn Curley wouldn't come off the field. We tried to get him off because I wanted to play Kenny Kennard and some of the younger kids. But Curley went right back out there. So did Elvin. Nope, by God, they wanted to stay. I'm proud of that. So, some good things can even come out of a defeat."

This would have been a logical time for Bum to attack the NFL playoff system which allows championship games to be played under inclement conditions such as January in Pittsburgh. A man from Houston would have a right to beef. No one would blame him for wanting to play such an important game in a warm-weather neutral site. But not Bum.

"I don't like neutral sites," he maintains. "Super Bowl is different. You don't know who's gonna play in it, and you've gotta know in advance or else TV coverage won't be good enough. They've got to have that hoopla, the hotel rooms and all that.

"But in the playoff games, I think one of the team's fans deserve the right to see their team play without it costin' them a helluva lot. In high school, we'd get in the playoffs and play teams 300, 400, 800 miles off. This state is big. People would want to meet us halfway, play at Ballinger or Austin or someplace. I'd say un-uh. The rules say both coaches got to agree on a neutral site or, otherwise, flip a coin. I flipped every time. I didn't want to make both their fans *and* our fans drive a long way.

"As bad as the weather was up there in Pittsburgh, the Pittsburgh fans deserved the right to see their football team. They had the best record. That's the rules of the game. Why should we want to change 'em just because the weather is bad? It's up to us to play better."

Bum was equally as understanding about Mike Wagner's game-ending hit on Mike Barber — after he talked to Terry Bradshaw.

"I believe Dan Rooney and I believe Chuck Noll, plus Terry has told me. If there is one guy on their football team that would not deliberately try to hurt somebody, it's Mike Wagner. He just would not do it. I think it was one of those cases that you could do it a billion times and nobody would hurt anybody. I think he and the other Steelers wanted our receivers to know they were there. That's part of football. Maybe he can't break it up but he lets you know that he's in that area.

"If I thought for a second that Wagner was doin' it to hurt Mike Barber, then I'd be very unhappy. But his intention was to hit Mike Barber; his damn intention was not to hurt Mike Barber. There's a difference."

The Oilers had been blown out of the water, so to speak, but they weren't about to alibi their way back to Houston.

"We wanted to run at them, try some play-action passes, keep the ball away from them, avoid having to make the big play," Pastorini told reporters after the game. "But the game plan went out the window the first half. You don't have a game plan when you're 31 points down.

"My feelings are one of remorse, one of regret, one of everything bad," Pastorini added. "I won't say we choked . . . we just got beat by the better team."

Bum reduced it to the simplest terms. "You have to look at everythin' square in the eye. They had their best day and we didn't."

To make matters worse, the Oilers were grounded for nearly five hours at the Greater Pittsburgh Airport because of the weather. Steelers 34, Oilers 5. Mike Barber's knee. Bum's hat. They couldn't get home fast enough.

A Party

What bothered Bum when the Oilers returned to Houston that night after losing so grossly to the Steelers was how embarrassing a "Welcome Home" party inside the cavernous Astrodome would be to the 2,000 or 3,000 die-hard fans who would show up.

After all, the team was arriving five hours late at the Houston airport. The final score was 34-5. All the cheering was on Mellon Square in Pittsburgh. Nevertheless, the Oilers were advised by officials at the Houston airport to board buses away from the main terminal for security reasons. That seemed strange. How dangerous was an empty airport?

"When I got out of the plane to get on a bus," Bum recalls, "Dan had a limousine waitin' and said 'Hell, come on and go with us.' Mauck and Barber got in, too. We all knew we were goin' to the Astrodome but we had no idea how many people were waitin' there. When you get beat as bad as we had, the only thing that's in your mind is 2,000 or 3,000 people. The limousine driver said, 'They got a helluva crowd at the Astrodome.' We said, 'Yeah, I bet.'

"Well, there had been 50,000 people out there since 5 p.m. We were supposed to get in there at 6 p.m., and now it was 11 p.m. We could see a helluva lot of cars when we drove up, like it was a football game, but we saw only one side of the Astrodome. In the back of my mind, I thought, 'Maybe this side is convenient and this is where everybody parked.' We never did know they were ringed all the way 'round the cotton-pickin' place.

"When you drive down the ramp into the Dome, you can see the field but you can't see the seats. The roof is blockin' your view. You can't see the seats until you get out of the car. Well, it was cotton-pickin' full. There was people in the aisles. Everybody went wild. But I'll tell ya, the fans did a heckuva job. They stayed in the stands. They did a whole lot better than the Pittsburgh fans.

"It's a helluva feeling to know that that many people would go to that much trouble. And believe me, it's some trouble to park at the Astrodome and walk through the cars and then sit there from 5 p.m. to 11 p.m. Now that is trouble, friend. I wouldn't do it. Hell's fire, I might wait and see 'em the next day or something. That is a lot of trouble to go through to welcome a football team that got beat."

Were those tears in Bum's eyes?

"I don't know," he shrugs. "Everybody says I cried. It was a stirrin' sight. I'll cry over a sad movie. I get involved in what I watch. I ain't necessarily ashamed of it and I ain't proud of it. It's just the way I am."

Bum was met on the floor of the Astrodome by sportscaster Anita Martini of radio station KPRC and asked to express his feelings to the fans.

"I couldn't hear what I was sayin' in there," Bum recalls. "But I told 'em Houston isn't a loser. Even though we had lost, we weren't losers. The fans weren't losers and the football players weren't losers. We had a good year and one game doesn't spoil a good year. Everybody went crazy. I mean I could not hear myself. Anything anybody said in the microphone, the fans went crazy again.

"That night I went home, talked to Helen for a little while and went to bed. Just normal. I always go to sleep and wake up the same time; it don't make any difference. I go to sleep between 11 o'clock and 1 o'clock every night and get up at 6:30 every mornin'. I used to go to coachin' clinics and we stayed up 'til 3 or 4 o'clock every mornin', seven nights in a row, and I woke up every damn mornin' same time. I just ain't one of them people that can sleep eight hours."

The beauty of Bum is that his boots change, but not him.

"If I could be remembered for one thing," Bum says, "that would be for bein' myself. You may not always be right but *do* what you think is right; and if you're wrong, have the ability to admit you're wrong. Both are damn important. Maybe you ain't got the market cornered on brains, but it's human nature to always want to be right."

Spoken like a real Bum.